The Runtons
Past and Present

Old & new images of East & West Runton

Researched and compiled
by members of the
Runton Parish History Society
www.runtonhistory.co.uk

ISBN 978-0-9561346-4-6

Published in 2012 by Red Flannel Publishing

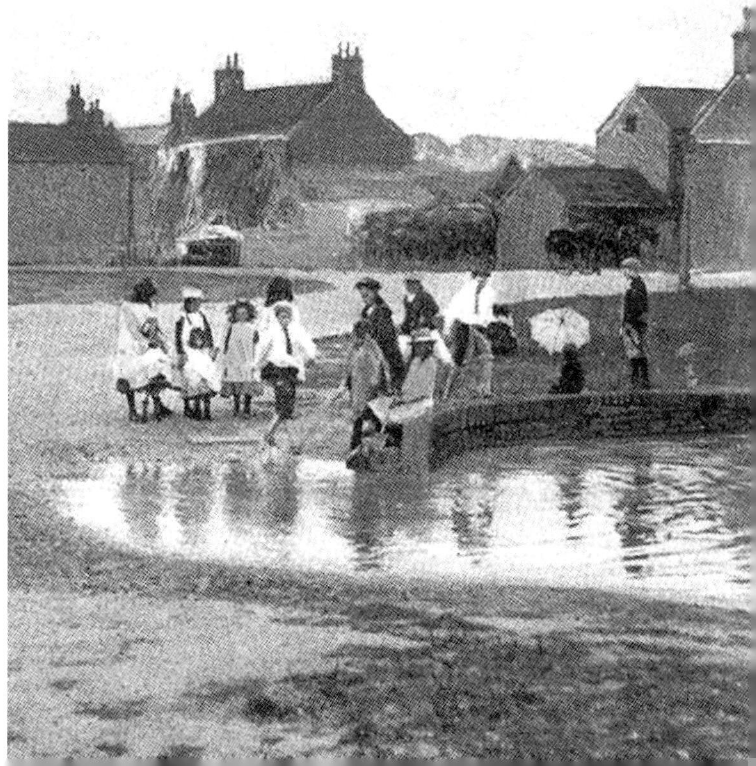

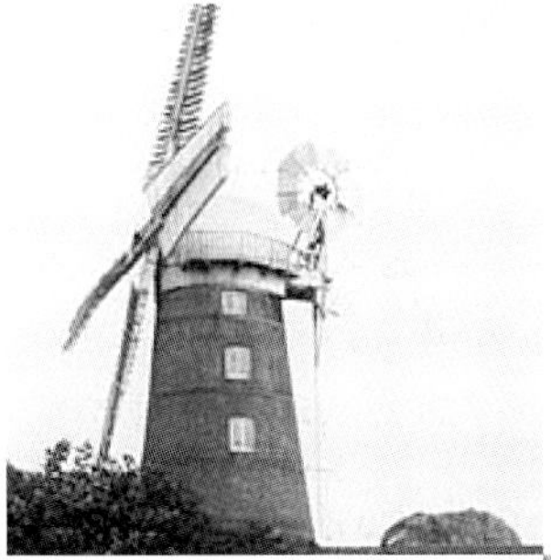

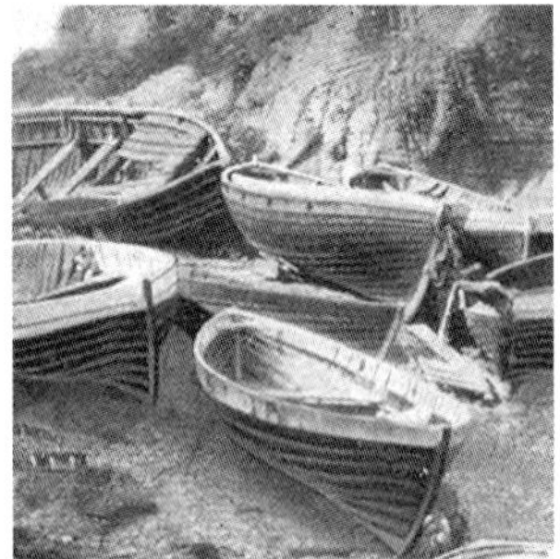

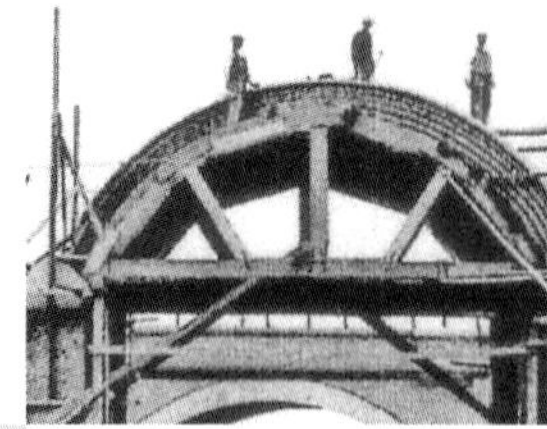

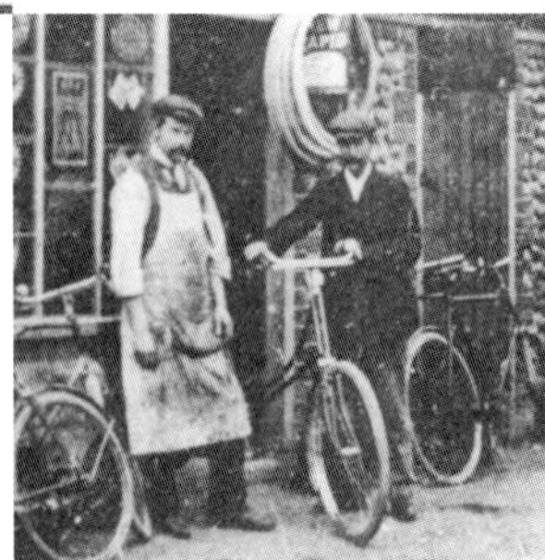

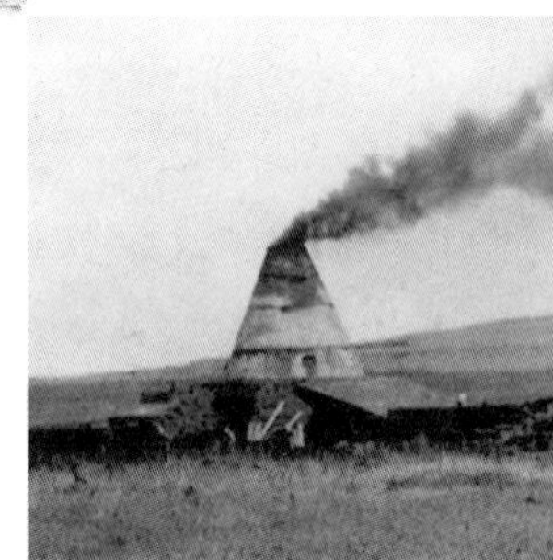

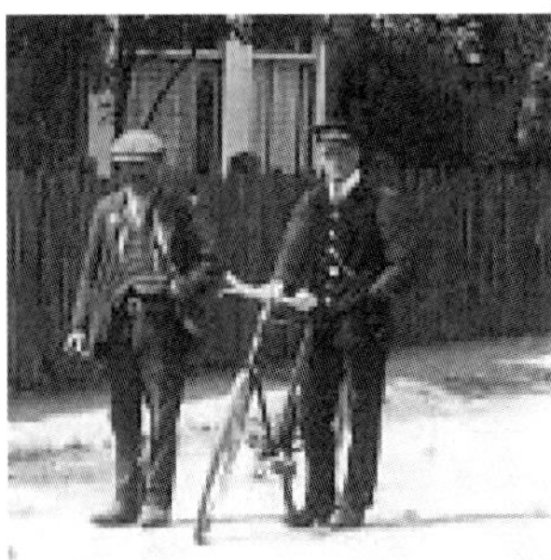

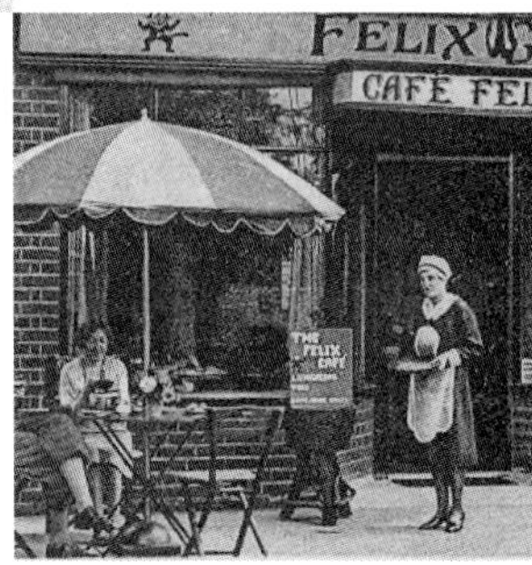
FELIX
CAFÉ FEL

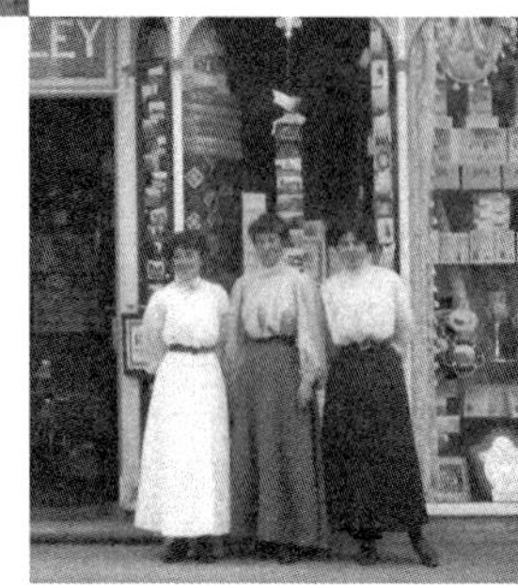
LEY

Introduction

In 2006 at a parish council meeting it was mentioned that during the previous year, fourteen elderly residents of East and West Runton had died, and with them so many memories of past village life. As a result, a committeee, later to become the Runton Parish History Society, was formed to investigate the possibility of collecting and collating photographs, documents, maps etc. Requests were made by way of posters, and newspaper appeals, and within a few months an amazing amount of material was donated. Being a coastal resort, there were numerous postcards obtained. Old maps and auction details were also unearthed. An appeal for holiday makers' memories was even published in The Leicester Mercury, resulting in a large number of responses. Within a few months, enough material was collected to enable a display, the first of many, to be held. One of the most popular displays has been the comparison of the villages in the past with the present day, hence this publication.

My thanks go to the numerous people who have contributed to our collection, which is still growing. I would also like to thank the members of the Runton Parish History Society who have contributed to this publication and in particular to John Creasey who has written the majority of the text, based on his own memories and incomparable knowledge of the Runtons.

Ray Spinks

Chairman

Runton Parish History Society

The Village Signs

The East Runton sign, with a carving showing a view from the beach looking up the Gap, was given in 1996 by Bob and Sue Wright in memory of their daughter Kelly Marie, who had been killed in a car accident the previous year, shortly after her marriage.

The West Runton sign was given by the Runton Women's Institute in 1977 to celebrate the Queen's Silver Jubilee, and unveiled by the singer Ian Wallace who had a home in the village. Originally it had a carved scene showing sheep grazing and the former brick kiln at Oxwell Cross. This decayed and has been replaced with a painted shield with village scenes, including the West Runton Elephant discovered in 1990.

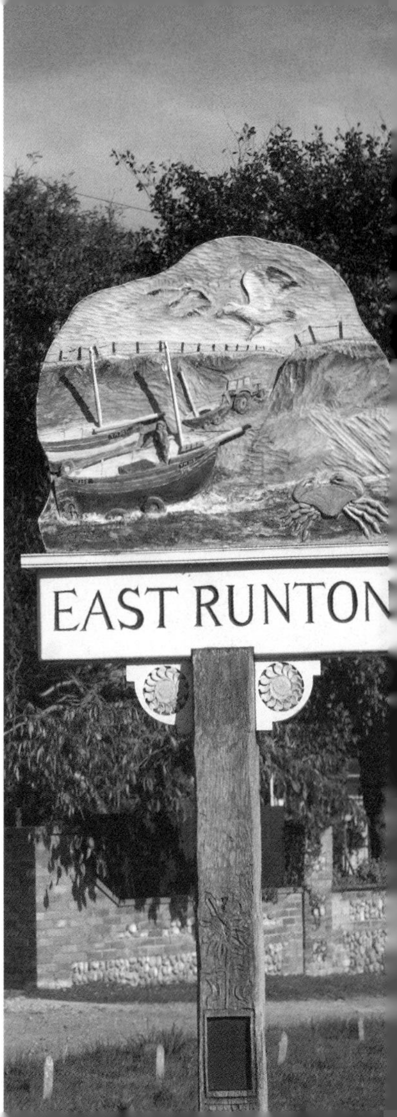

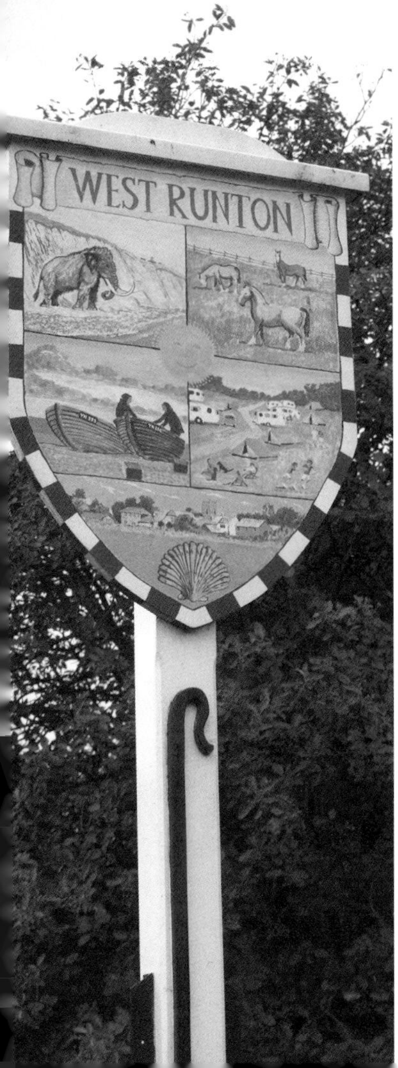

Censuses

The government censuses from 1841 to 1911 have provided a considerable amount of information. For instance, the 1871 census reveals that in the parish there were 45 agricultural labourers, 40 fishermen and 17 farmers. How many of those occupations would we find today? Amongst the occupations listed were nine domestic servants, a shepherd's boy aged 12, a rat catcher, a washerwoman, a shoemaker and a cordwainer. The shoemaker was in fact a cobbler, who mostly repaired shoes, whilst a cordwainer actually manufactured footwear, a wheelwright and two blacksmiths. The more unusual occupations included a "sick nurse and bible reader", and the "matron of an orphan asylum". The population of the Parish at this time was about 500, a large proportion being children. Many households comprised families totalling as many as eight, and sometimes more. Quite a handful when you remember that a large number of the houses were just "two up and "two down".

At the end of the 19th century the railways were being built and the viaducts were being constructed at East Runton. Many of the farmworkers defaulted from their jobs and went to work on the railways and bridges because the pay was better.

A view of the High Street, East Runton, probably 1910-1913 and most certainly out of season, with four people only to be seen. It is all much tidier than now, though the iron railings were taken away for the war effort in the 1940's. All the buildings are still there, except a small property which can be just seen adjoining Flint House and some buildings beyond the turning of Felbrigg Road on the left. Munday's shop has well-filled windows and boards outside. A small shed in the yard of the White Horse is also long gone.

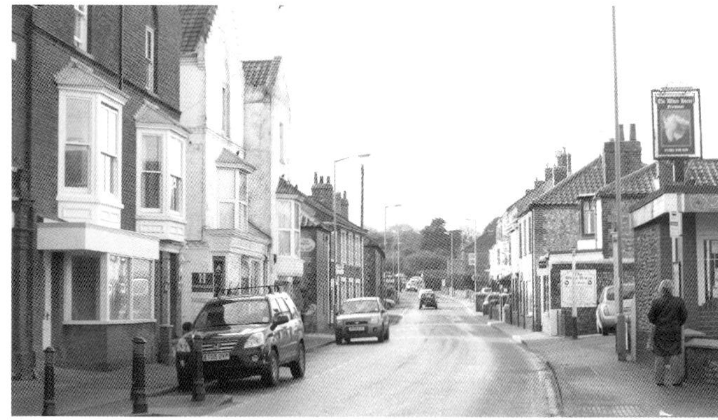

The recent view shows alterations to some buildings, new shop-fronts and notices. There is a new building on the immediate right, replacing another small shop not built at the time of the former view. There is now street lighting, new pavements, parking places and a controversial crossing place on the south side of the street. Traffic in February, when this photograph was taken, is not what it is in the summer months.

East Runton - High Street

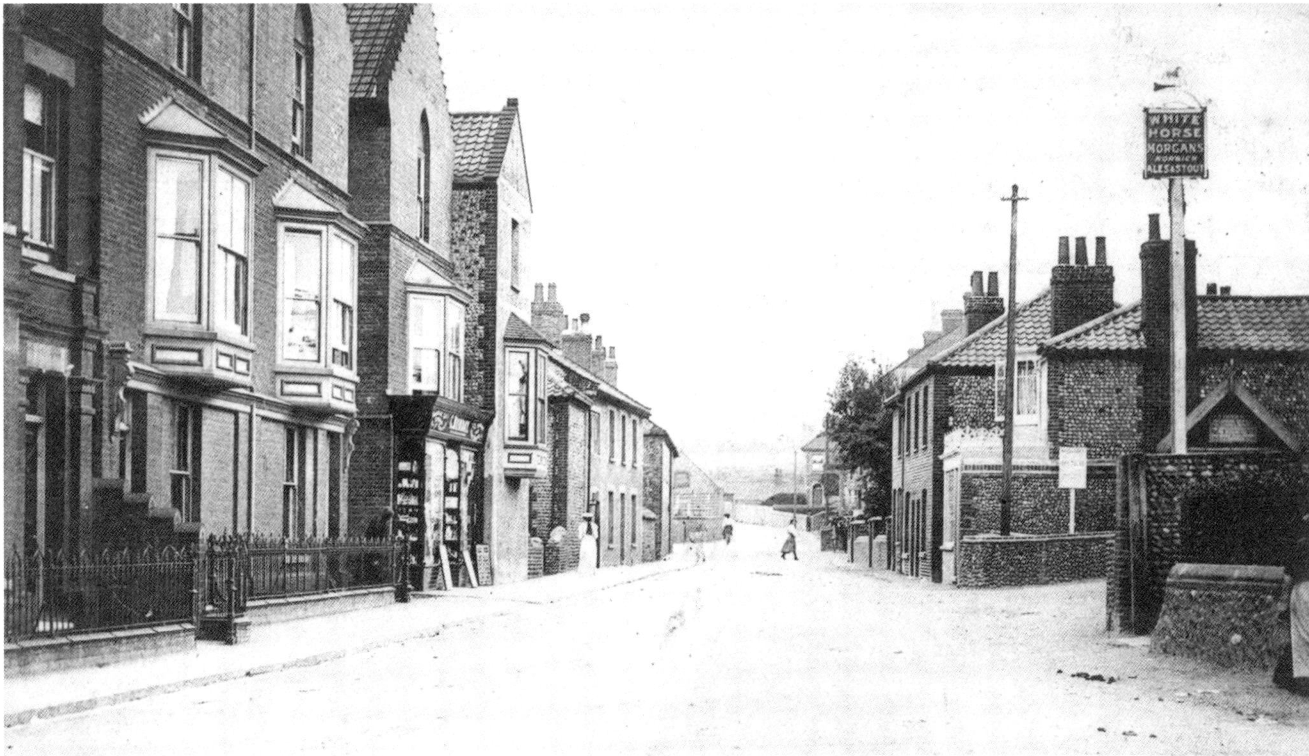

This photograph shows a view of the Street (Cromer Road) in the early 1900's, before two bays of the old farmhouse, the long building on the left, were taken down to enable an extension to be made to the house on the immediate left of the view. Beyond the farmhouse are stables, now two cottages, and next the large window of the then grocer's shop. Across the road is the wall in front of West Runton House, with the trees which sheltered it from the road. Beyond is the glebe field wall, where the present Rectory was built in 1929, and then a glimpse of the churchyard. Artfully posed are a man with a barrow and a lady and gent with bicycles.

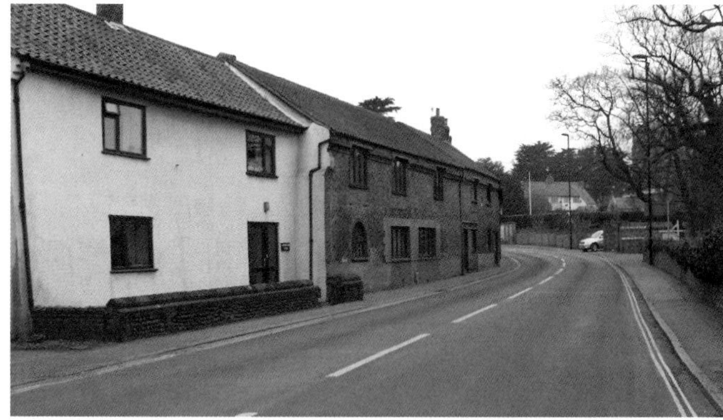

As with many of these photographs the striking change is the creation of what is now the busy A149 road. It would be interesting if one could compare what travelled along the road in an hour at the time of the photograph opposite, compared with today. Certainly the lady would not be able to wheel her bicycle in the middle of the road now.

West Runton - Cromer Road

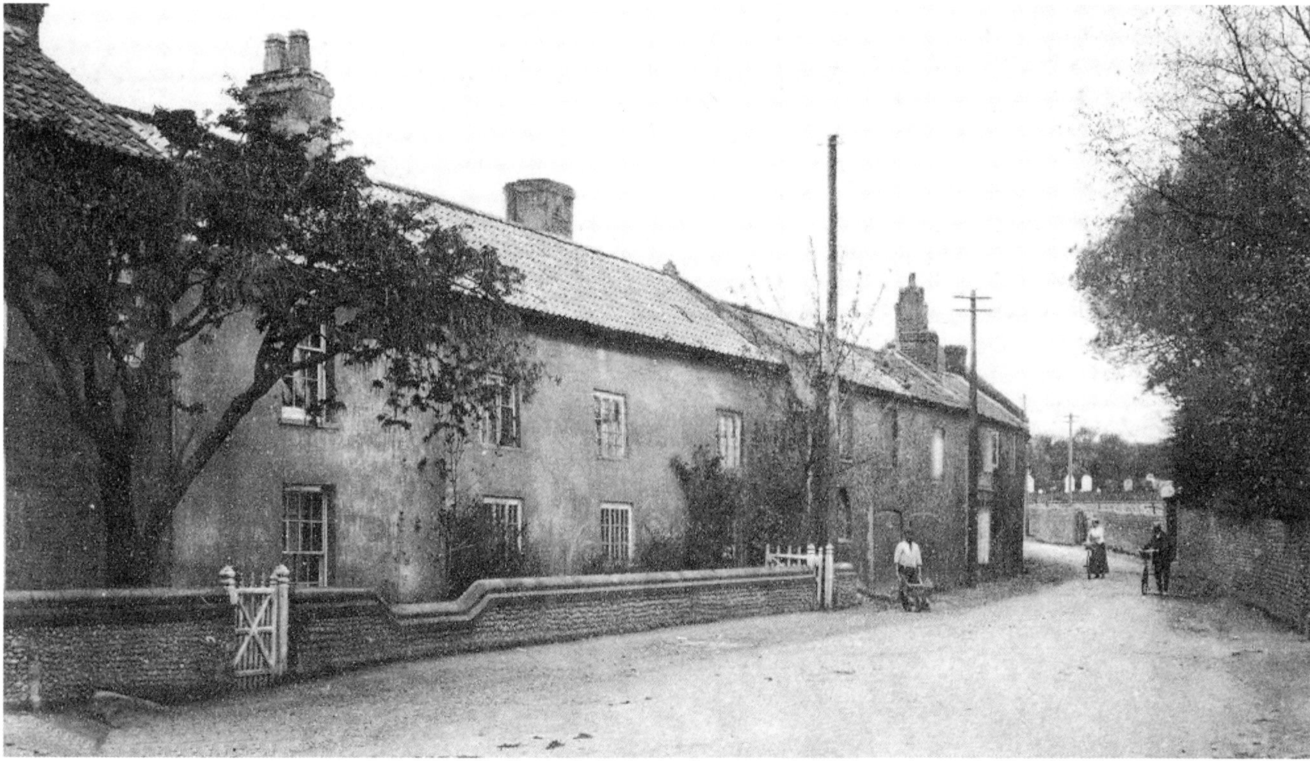

Frederick Weaights, the owner of the cycle shop was born at Itteringham, Norfolk, in 1884. He came to East Runton and established his business around 1902, living nearby in Victoria Terrace. He is seen here in work apron outside his first premises, which he later replaced with a brick and timber building on the same site, with doors opening to the road, and later diversified into selling petrol. He sold his business, with a load of obsolete stock, and his house to E. B Hodson in late 1947, and moved to another house. He died in 1970, having been blind for some years. He was one of the characters of the village. Under its new owner the business became a motor garage and was later rebuilt when part was removed for road widening.

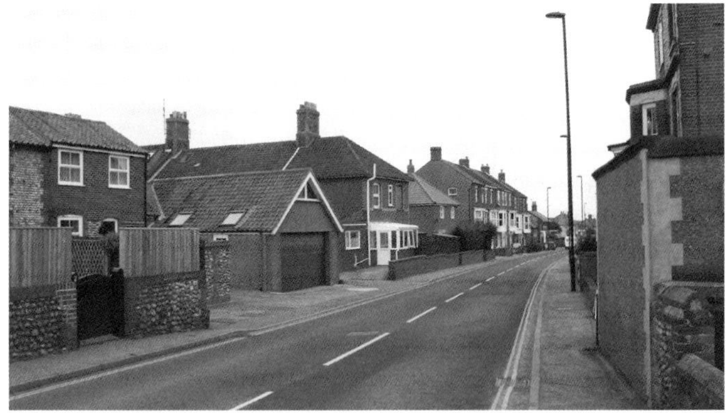

Frederick Weaights cycle shop would have stood where the garage is located on the left hand side of the A149 as it enters East Runton from the west. The original building would have projected further into what was a much smaller and of course quieter road.

East Runton - Cycle Shop

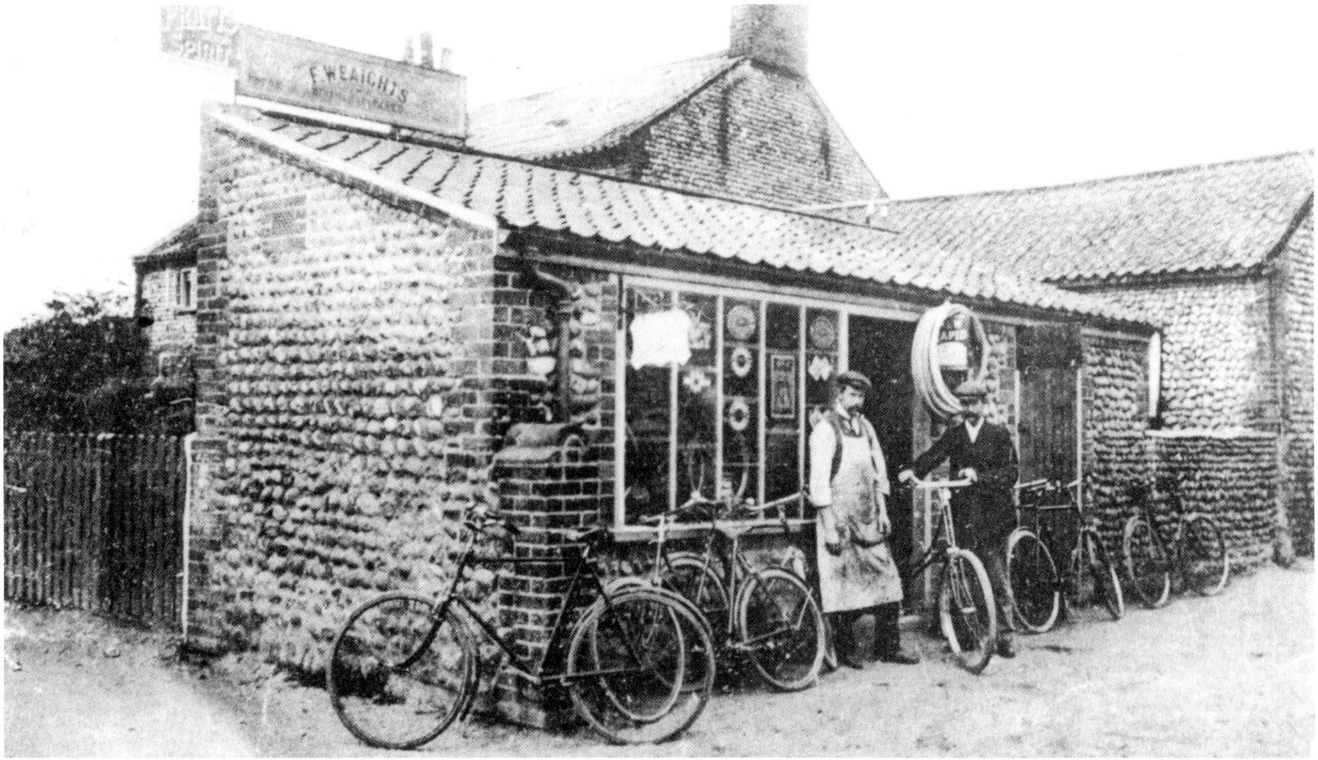

This property was built in the mid-1920's and here Herbert Payne opened his first drug store before moving to new premises in the Street and qualifying as a pharmacist. The Felix Cafe was run by the two Misses Smallman and there was a tea garden at the side. It closed in 1939. The proprietors returned after the war for a short time but the Cafe did not then reopen. It did subsequently for a while and was later a dress shop, known as Yvonne, run by a Mrs Fox from Renwick Park. Then was a bread and cake shop and after the Wedgwood Restaurant. At the end of 1973 Manfred Hollwoger opened it as the Mirabelle Restaurant, enlarging it in 1976 and later. The Mirabelle had a wide reputation for excellence. Manfred retired and closed it in 2005, and the property was sold to a builder. The restaurant re-opened in 2006, but not for long.

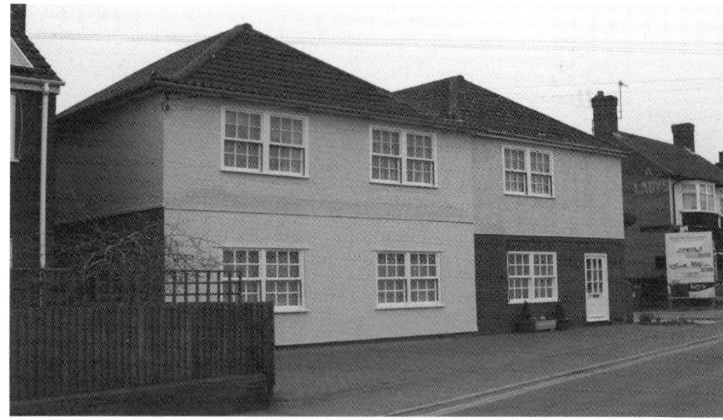

The building has now been converted into apartments and three properties have been built in the grounds. The uniformed waitress and the holiday-makers enjoying afternoon tea in the early view make a period scene of around 1930.Today the Felix Cafe is unrecognisable. it is the part of the building with four windows and no door. The part to the right with a white door is a later extension.

West Runton - Felix Cafe

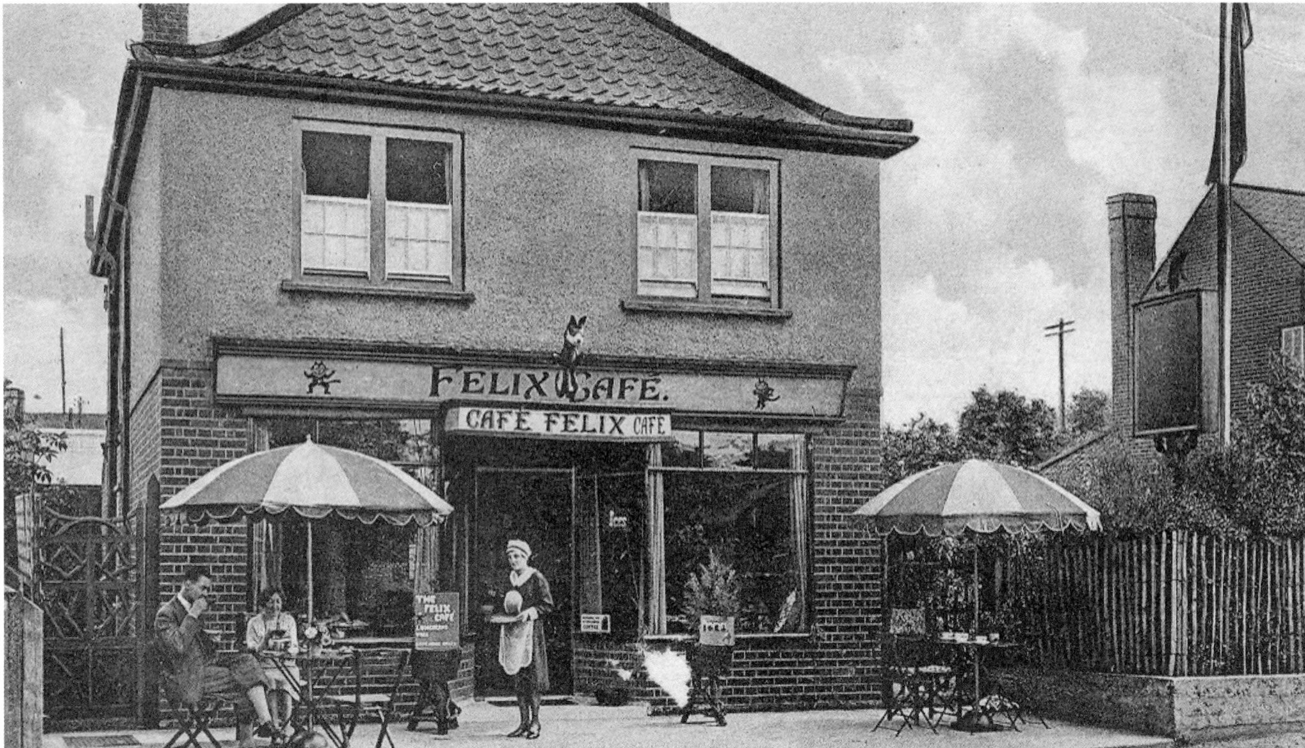

Herbert Fox was here in 1888, succeded by 1892 by Thomas Puxley, who was also in Cromer. His son, William, has taken over the East Runton shop by 1900 and let apartments in the season (six bed and two sitting rooms). In summer evenings with her work over, Mrs Puxley would go to the beach with her assistants for a paddle in the sea. The business was sold in the mid 1940's and has since had a succession of owners. "Puxleys" was a village institution and Mr Puxley had a great knowledge of, and care for, his customers.

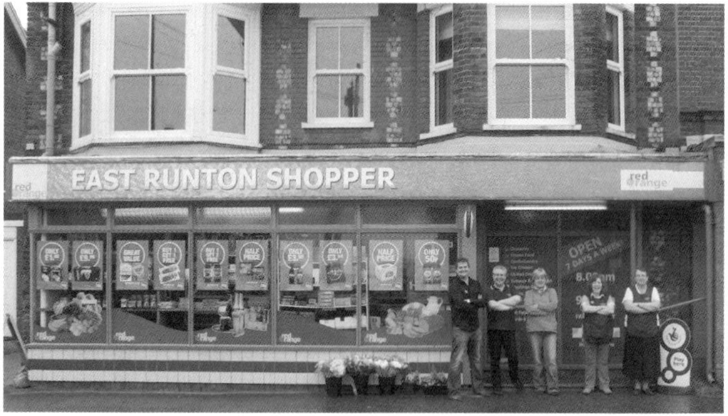

We are pleased to report that the shop is still thriving under the ownership of Steve and Tammy Bacon, having now extended into the adjoining building. The layout and style of the shop reflects the modern way of self service, but in this case we can say that personal service also continues to be present. Throughout this book we show the then and now in terms of buildings and landscape, but this is the one place that we are able to show the change in terms of clothes and fashion.

East Runton - The Draper, Grocer & Provision Merchant

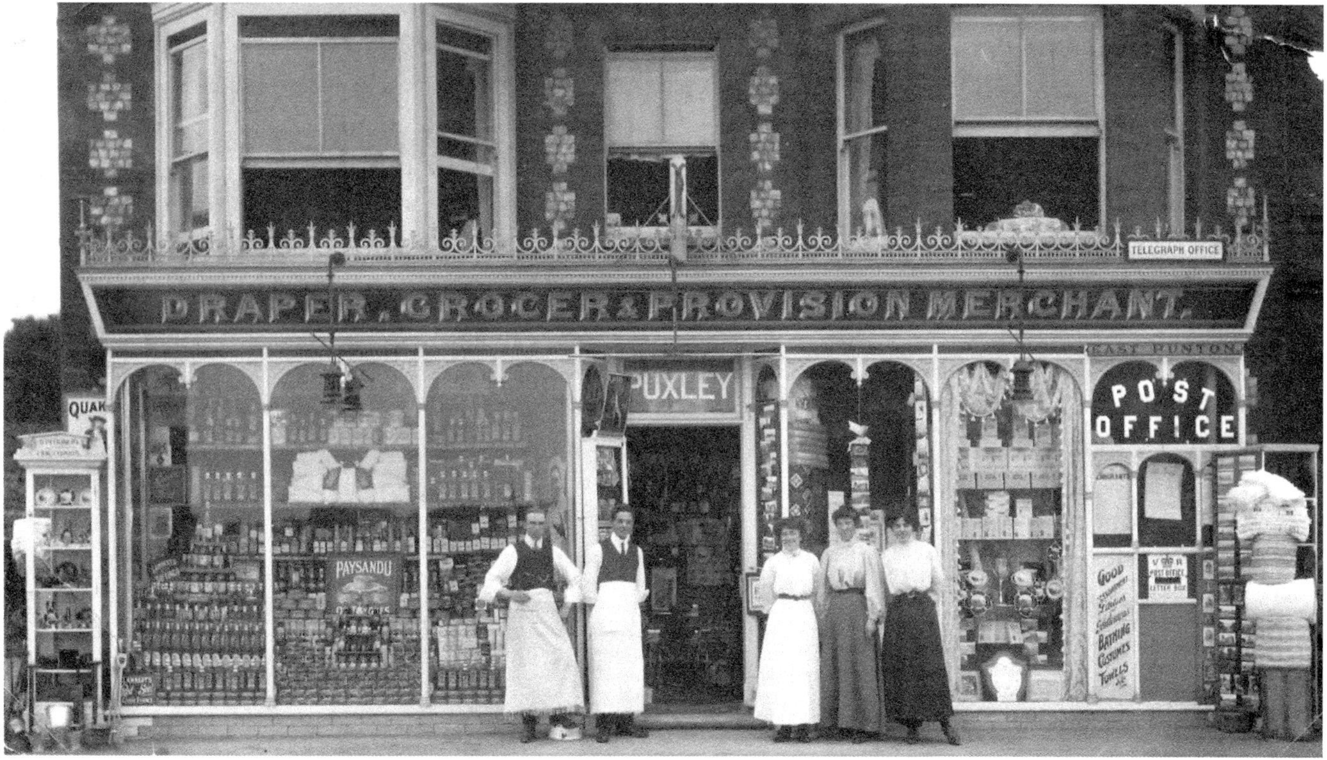

A view of Cromer Road in West Runton from the early 1950's. On the left is Threeways Cafe, and beyond that is an old Farmhouse, with a board saying Laburnum Farm Dairy - although it is illegible in the photograph. Next to this is a road sign with a torch, proclaiming a school in the vicinity, Runton Hill School (now the Kingswood Centre). Beyond the telephone pole, the door of the barn/stable next to the farmhouse is open. Beyond can be seen the parish church and the garden wall of the Rectory. Trees hide Runton House from the road, a notice board amongst them advertises the West Runton Hotel. The Post Office was then in the former lodge to Runton House, to which it moved around 1937. A van and a car stand outside, the car has the registration JLY 265.

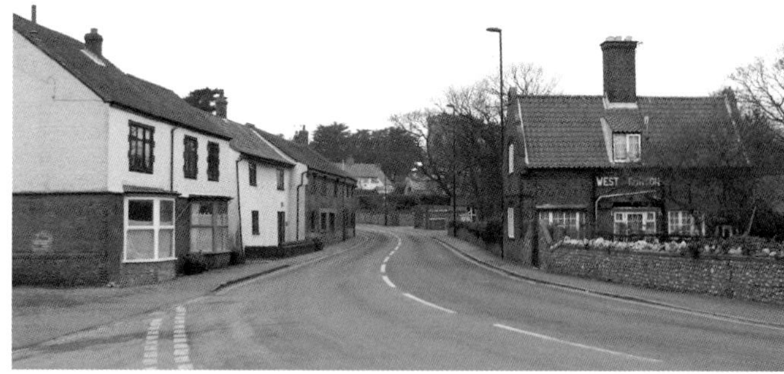

The recent view is not markedly different, though the Threeways Cafe and the Farmhouse are now private houses and the further farm buildings have been converted into houses. Street lights replace the telephone pole. The Lodge is again a private house. When the Post Office moved to the bungalow on the corner of Station Road the lettering "Post Office" was removed from the Lodge but "West Runton" was allowed to remain. Some people wonder why it is there.

West Runton - Cromer Road

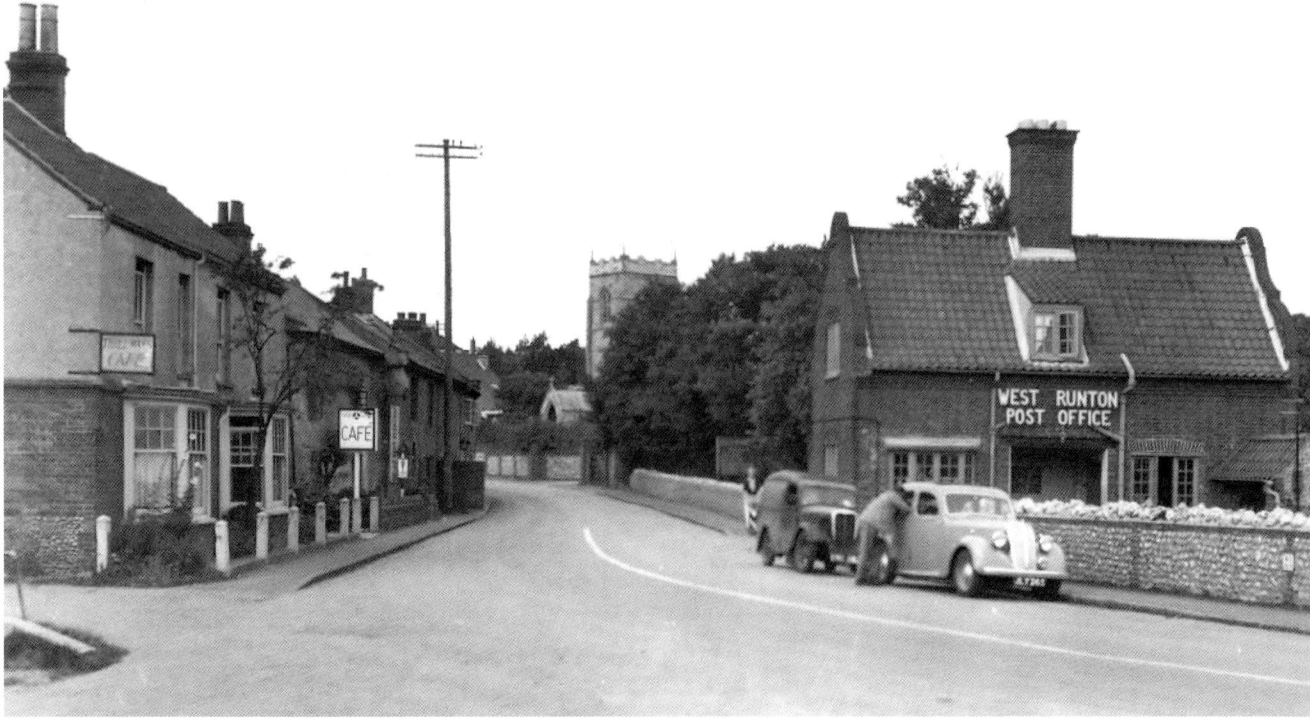

A peaceful scene from the first decade of the twentieth century, before the pair of houses to the immediate west of the church were built around 1909. We see the gable end of one of the Church Cottages, built in 1869. West Runton's first Post Office was in the centre cottage. On the south side of the road is a wall belonging to the Church Farm.

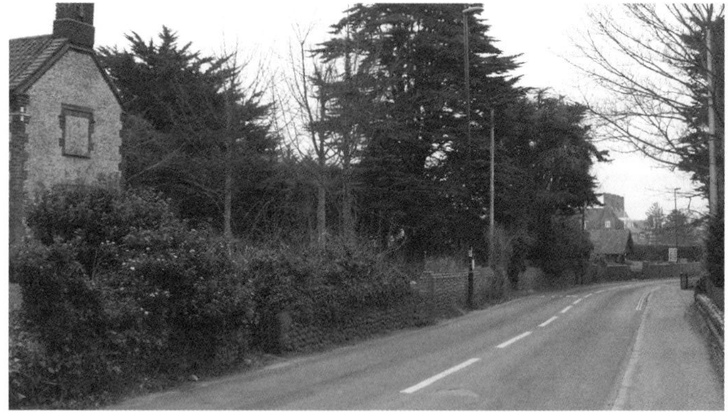

In some respects this scene has changed little in the past hundred years, the cottage on the left is immediately identifiable. The wall along the left hand side is still there but covered in vegetation. The church is of course hidden behind the large trees. The main difference is that the wall on the south side of the road has been demolished to allow for subsequent road widening and pavement.

West Runton - The Church

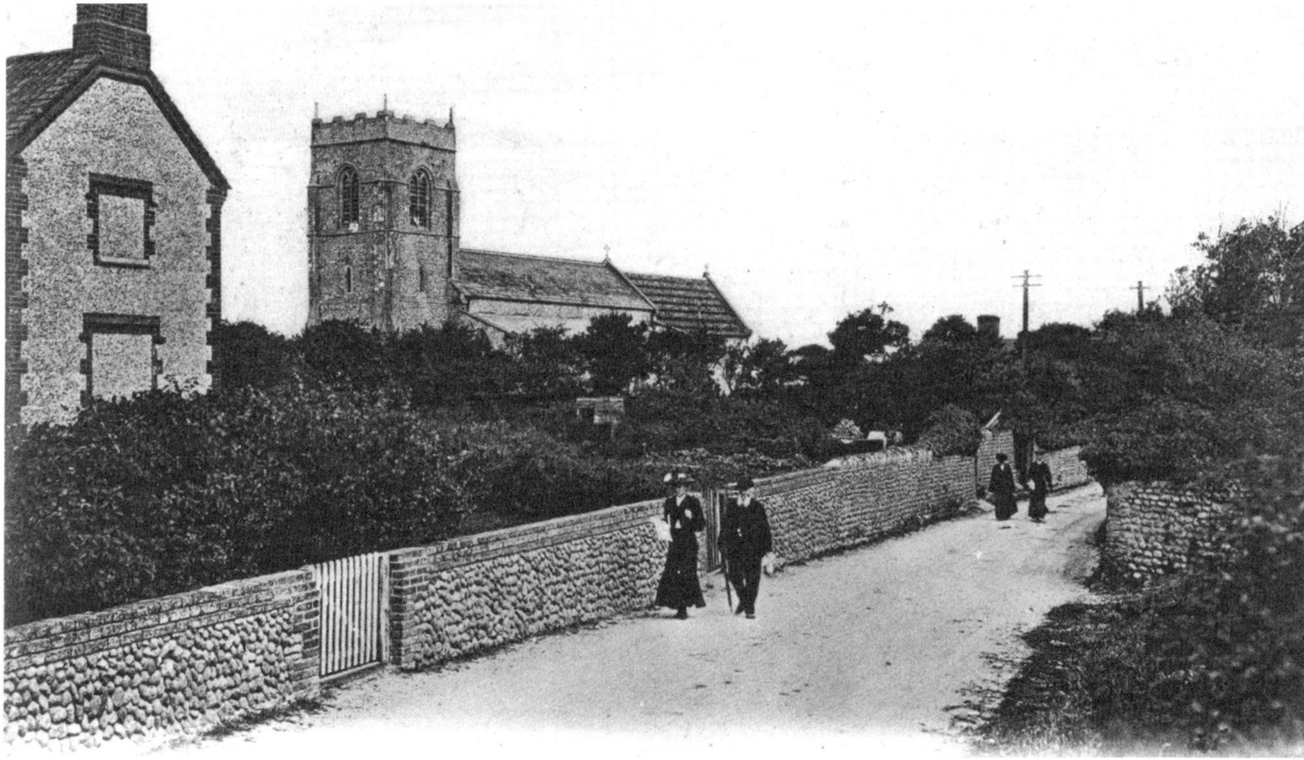

This view of West Runton's main street dates from the mid-1950's. There are telegraph poles to be seen but no street lighting. The lay-by in front of the grocer's shop had not been made. The black and white post of the bus stop sign can be seen on the pavement. The furthermost shop, then Bertram Reynolds, has boards outside against the Chapel wall advertising coach trips from Sheringham. Then comes the tall grocer's shop, then F Harrington and next to that the bread shop, with a "Hovis" sign; then a ladies' hairdresser and Herbert W Payne M.P.S., the chemist. Finally, and partly off the picture, F.G.Lines, Confectioner, Fruiterer and Newsagent. The blind across the lower part of his window has an advertisement for Wills' tobacco. Across the road can be seen the end of Arthur's butcher's shop. The star on the pole of the Inn sign reads: Caravan Site. The car number appears to be DVF 148.

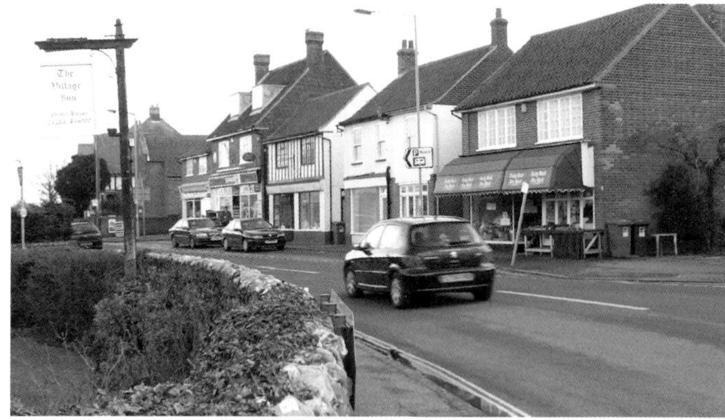

Today the view is still very much the same. The Inn sign now hangs across the garden. The furthest shop now sells caravan accessories, the grocer's is the Spar Store incorporating the Post Office. The bread shop is now a cafe, the hairdressers has closed and is currently empty, The chemist's shop closed in 1970 and what was the shop has been incorporated into the house behind.

West Runton - Cromer Road

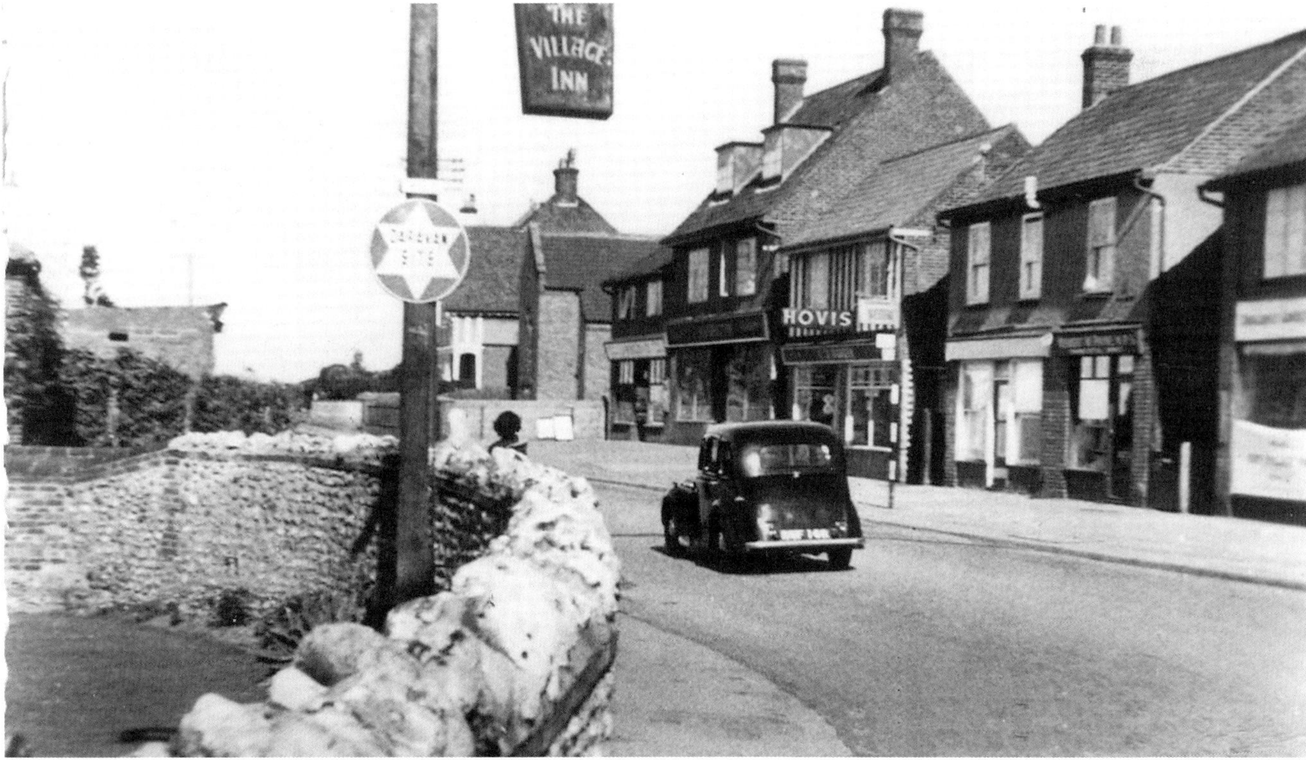

The Post Office at West Runton has had numerous locations. This view is no later than 1906, before the building was extended with another house to the west. The then postmaster was J. W. Payne, who advertised Confectioner and Refreshments. The curved displays on his window advertise Cadbury's Chocolate. There were then no houses in the lower part of Station Road and to the far left can be seen the gable of houses in Rosebery Road. The area in front of the shop was then bare of grass and on the Common in front was a pond, fed by the streams which come down from the hills behind the village. It was filled in many years ago but water can still collect here after a heavy shower. The stream, which once emerged here before going under the road and into the garden of the Village Inn (opened in 1927) was covered in during the 1960's. Not for nothing was the row of cottages on the right known jocularly as "Mud Row".

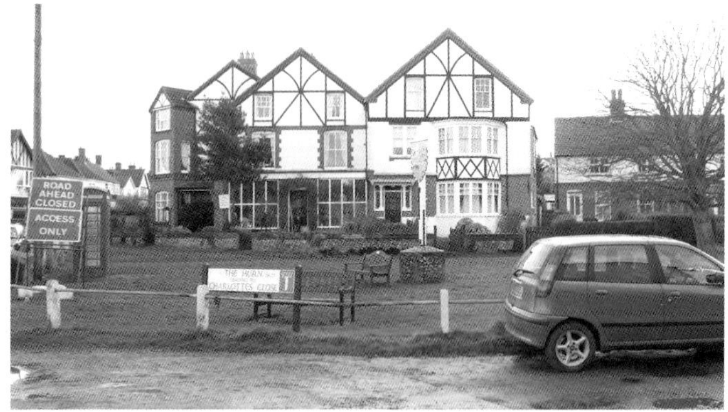

This recent photograph shows numerous changes. The telephone kiosk was moved to the Common from the side of the Chapel wall around 1950. The posts around the Common were first erected around 1920. The village sign was first erected in 1977 by the W.I. to commemorate the Queen's Silver Jubilee. One can of course contrast the parked car with the pony and trap in the early photograph.

West Runton - Post Office

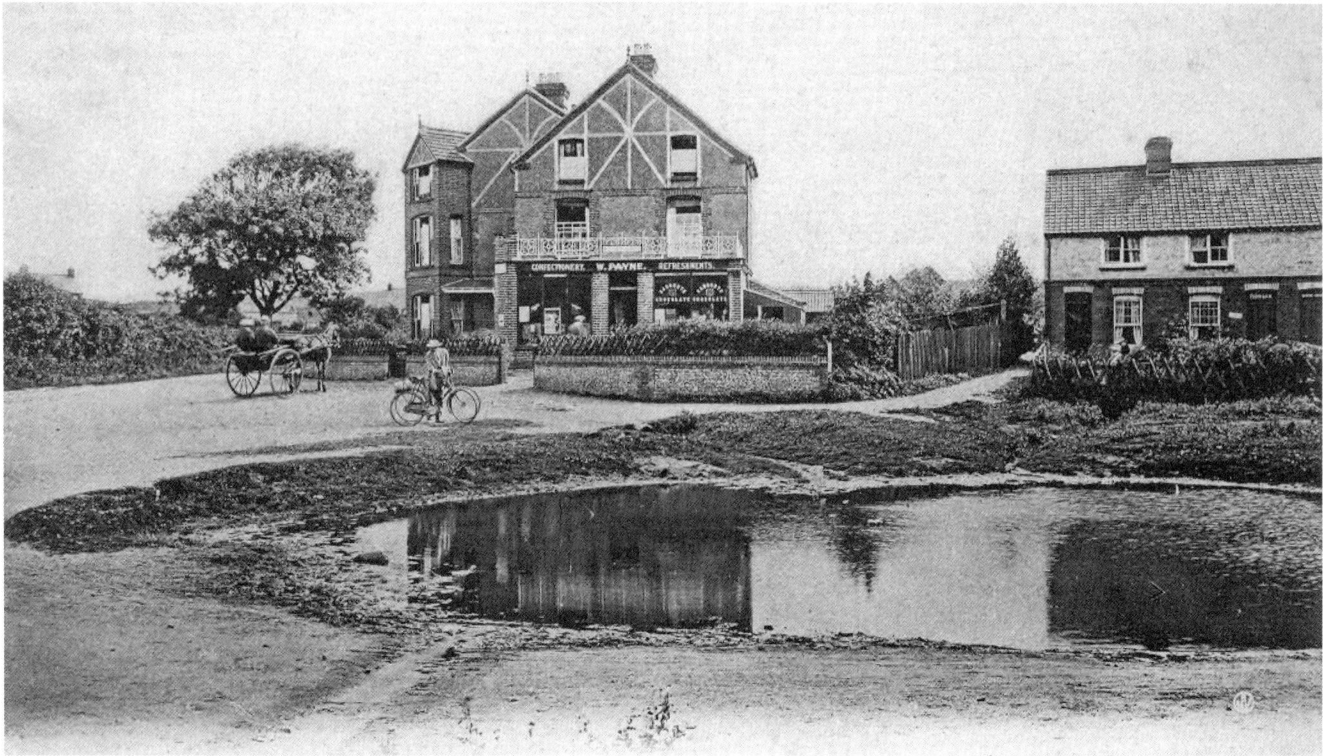

Opposite is one of the earliest postcards of West Runton. Printed in Dresden, Germany, it is no later than 1903. The pair of cottages in the centre have been one house for many years. To the left is the gable of the house on the corner of The Hurn. To the right is a chimney of West Runton House and then the buildings belonging to it converted into the Village Inn in 1927 and the house, then two cottages, at the top of Water Lane.

To the left of the church can be seen, on the skyline, Eden Lodge, in which Runton Hill School began in 1911, and then the Church Farm House with the Church Cottages behind it. The farm buildings below have gone and the history of the former railway carriages is forgotten. A lady with a small trap, perhaps hired from a local jobmaster, completes the picture.

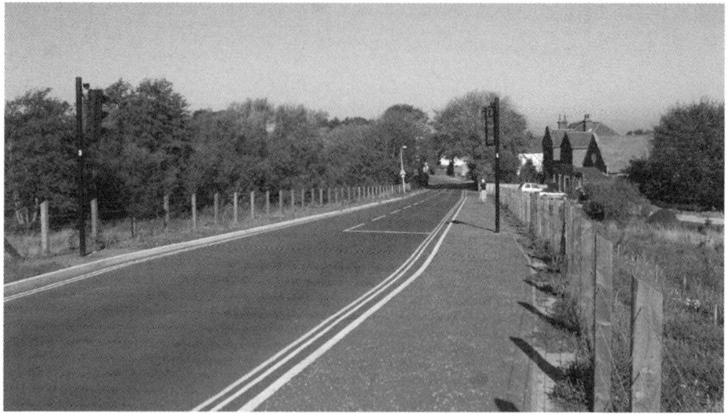

Today the scene looks much less interesting. This section of road has recently been resurfaced and the traffic lights introduced as part of the railway bridge improvement project. All the original buildings are still there, but are hidden behind the trees which have grown up in the intervening 100+ years.

West Runton - looking north from the railway bridge

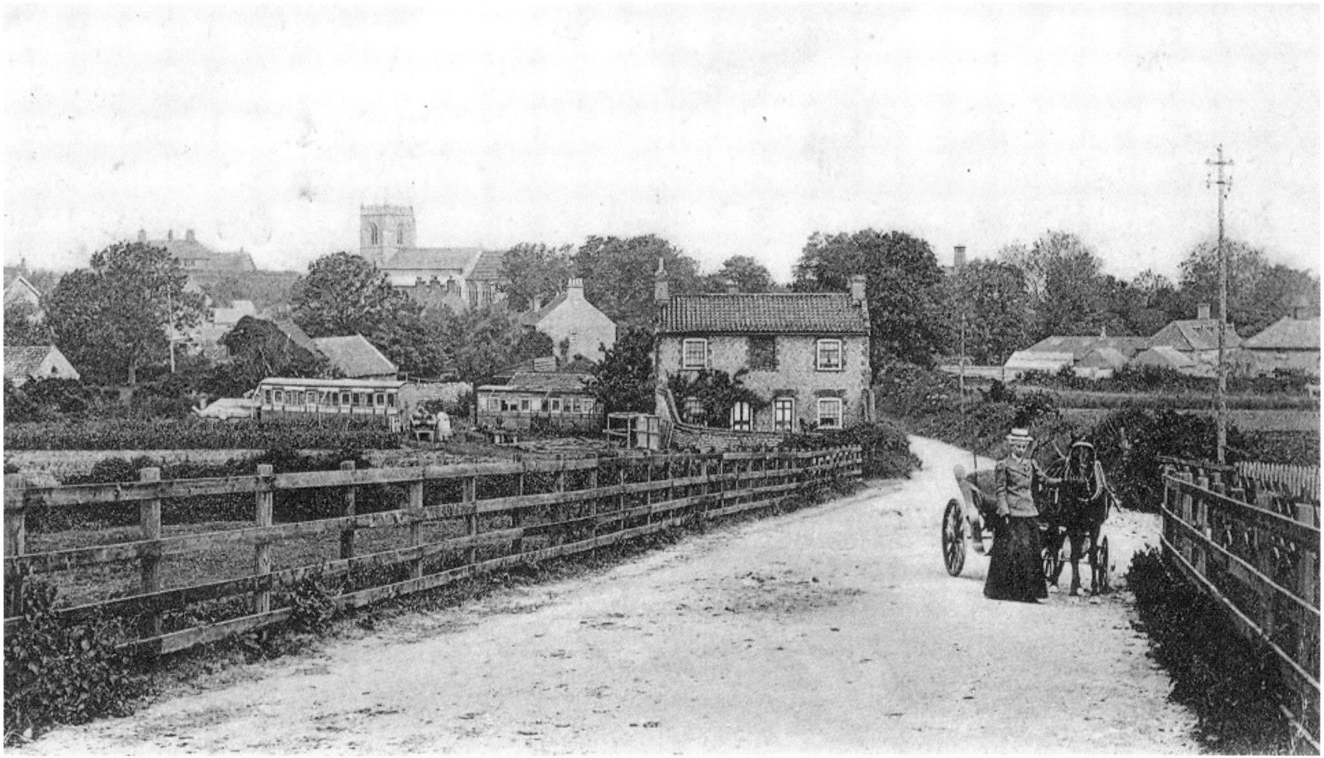

This photograph probably dates from around 1913. The Links Hotel was built in 1899, on to an existing house known as Woodlands, which can be seen on the left. In the centre is the house once known as Sea View. To the right is the former Cecil House, dated 1891, now Tapdon House, built on the site of a much earlier building.

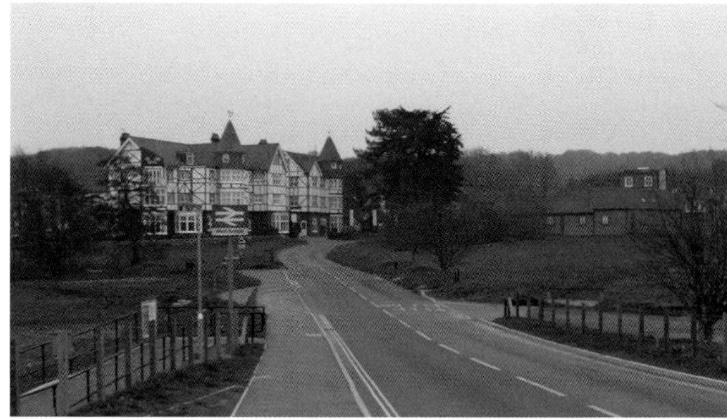

The view from the railway bridge looking south has changed little in a hundred years. The Links Hotel has been extended, the roadway has been widened and surfaced and trees have grown, but the man with the horse and cart would easily recognise where he was if he came back today.

West Runton - looking south to the Links Hotel

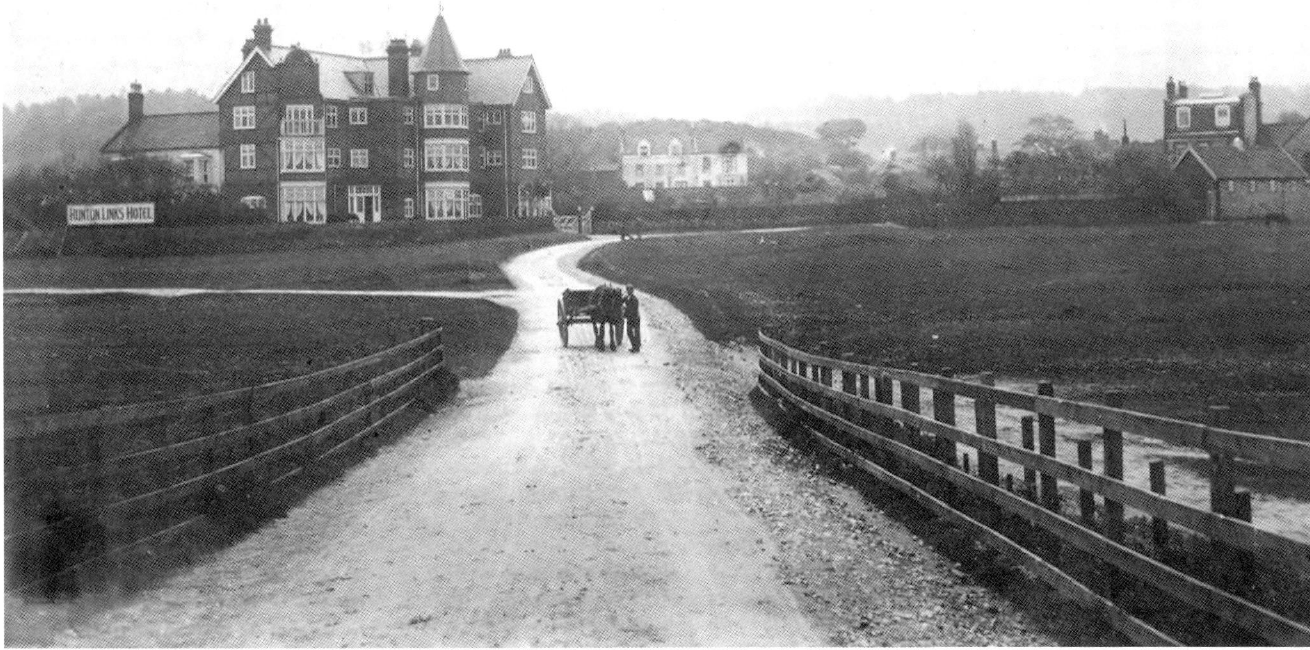

The photograph opposite was taken from the balcony of one of the north facing rooms of the Links Hotel, built in 1899. It would have been taken by 1903 and shows a wider panorama than the view taken from the railway bridge. On the left can be seen Orchard Cottages, now with alterations, and with other properties to the south and beyond. Eden Lodge and the church stand out. West Runton House is hidden in the trees but its lodge can be seen. On the right is Sir Fowell Buxton's Mission Room, built in 1900, now the Church Hall.

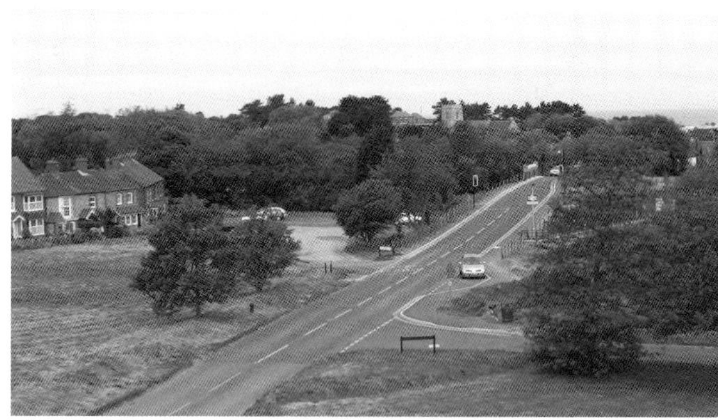

We were fortunate in being able to access the very same hotel room to take the present day photograph. The scene is immediately recognisable, but as with many of the present day images much of the view is obscured by the proliferation of trees. Fortunately the church still stands above them to give a point of reference.

West Runton - looking north from the Links Hotel

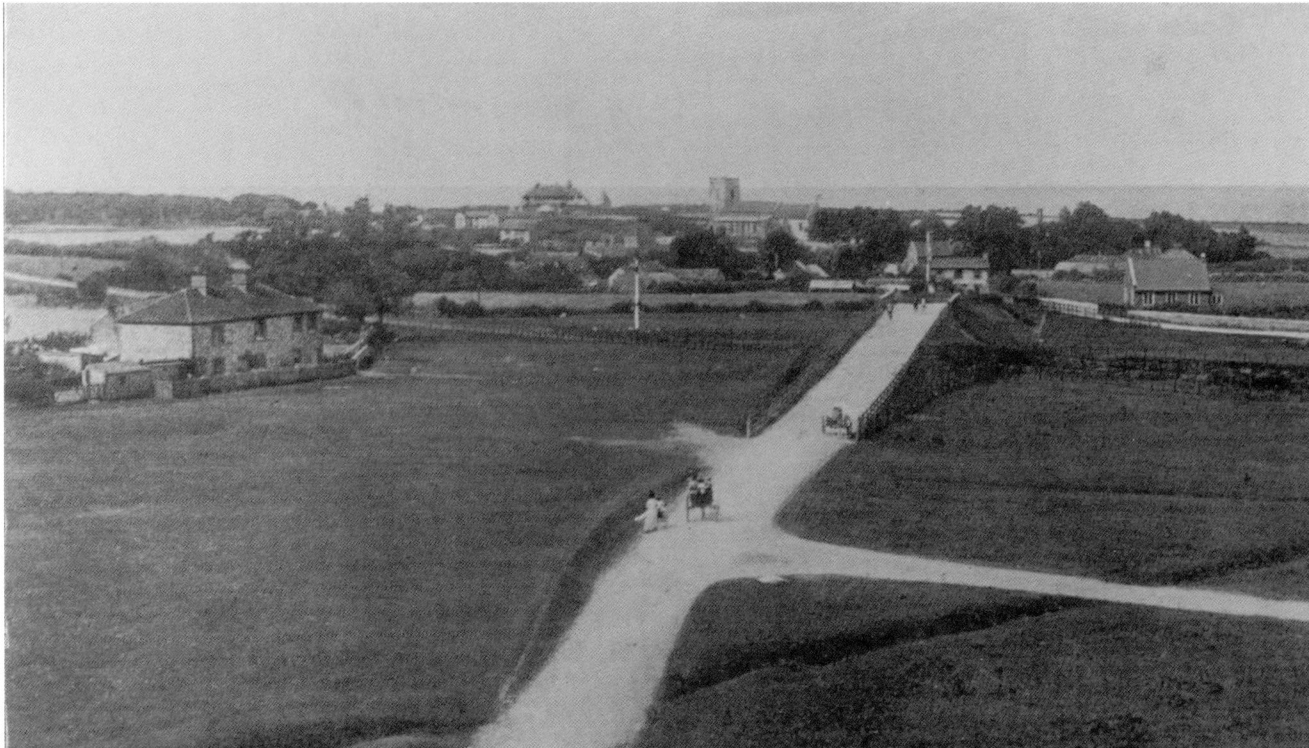

A mid to late 1920's view (judging by the ladies' hats) looking south. One wonders who the gentleman striking an attitude in the middle of the road was. The pavement on the left is raised and carries the stream under it which then turns right and makes its way to the beach. The houses on the right, and Newell Crescent behind them, are on land that was formerly the grounds of West Runton House. Plots in Water Lane were advertised for sale in 1921.

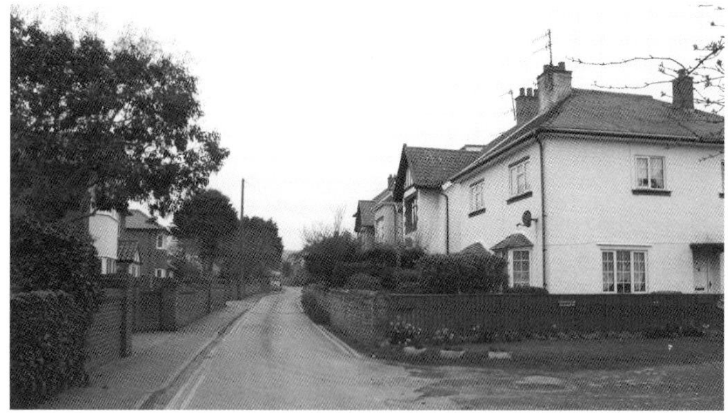

The main change here has been the demolition of the wall on the far right of the picture, to create an access to what is now Newell Crescent. Water Lane has not been widened over the years and the recent photograph appears to be the only one in this book where there are actually fewer trees than in the corresponding early photograph.

West Runton - Water Lane

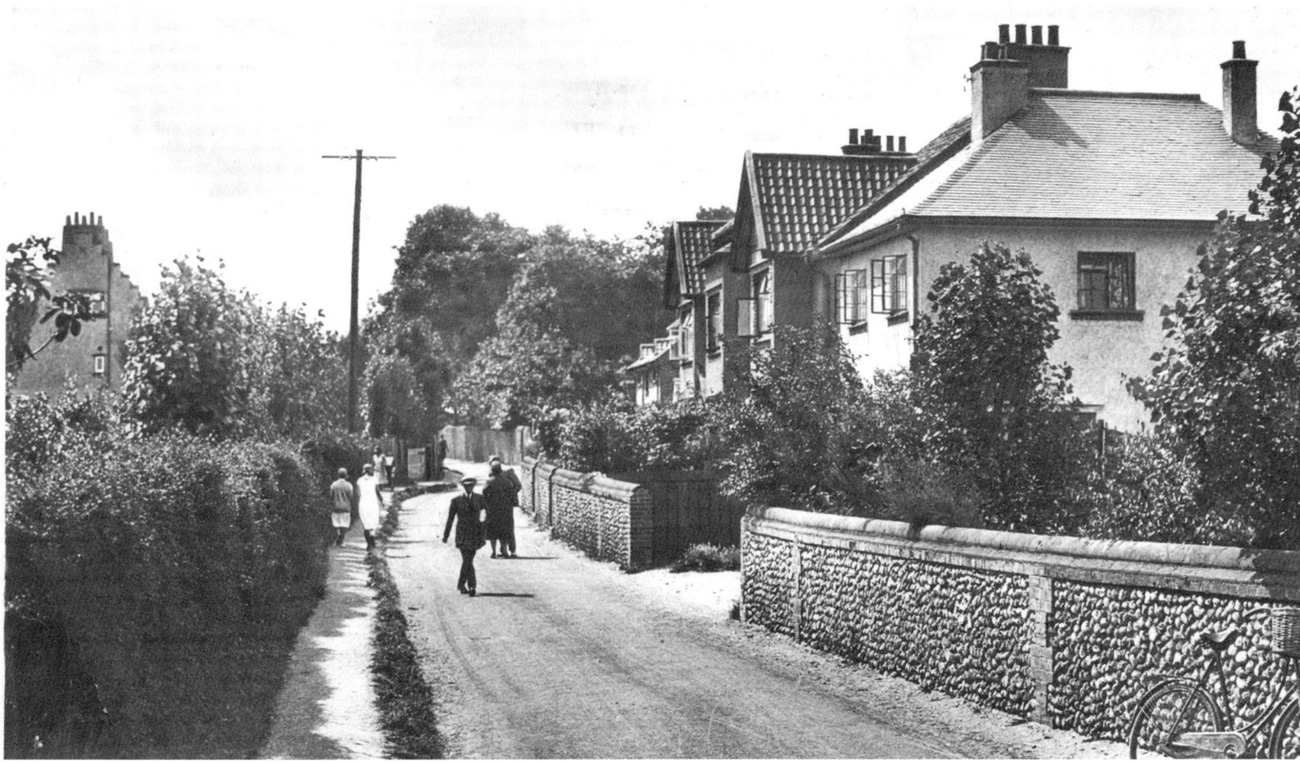

This photograph taken in the 1960's shows the Caravan Club site in the foreground, the golf course, with the road across it, in the middle distance and a fine view of West Runton beyond taken from Incleborough Hill. The growth of trees on the hillside prevented the exact replication of the photograph which showed all three elements. While it cannot be seen in today's photograph, the caravan site is thriving as caravaning becomes ever more popular. The Links Hotel golf course also continues to be popular. The course was opened in 1903 as a 9 hole course, extended to 18 holes by 1906. During the 1939-45 War it became an army assault course and was re-opened, after reconstruction, in 1949. The Club closed in 1953 and part of the course was subsequently sold. The course re-opened around 1960 and in 1963 became the present 9 hole course

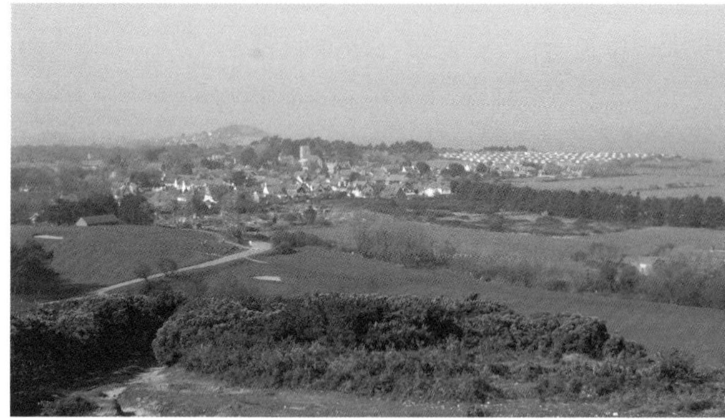

Incleborough Hill which lies between East and West Runton is one of the highest in Norfolk and provides exceptional views over both villages. This view looks west across West Runton, the church clearly stands out and Beeston Bump at Sheringham can be seen in the distance.

West Runton - Looking across the campsite and golf course

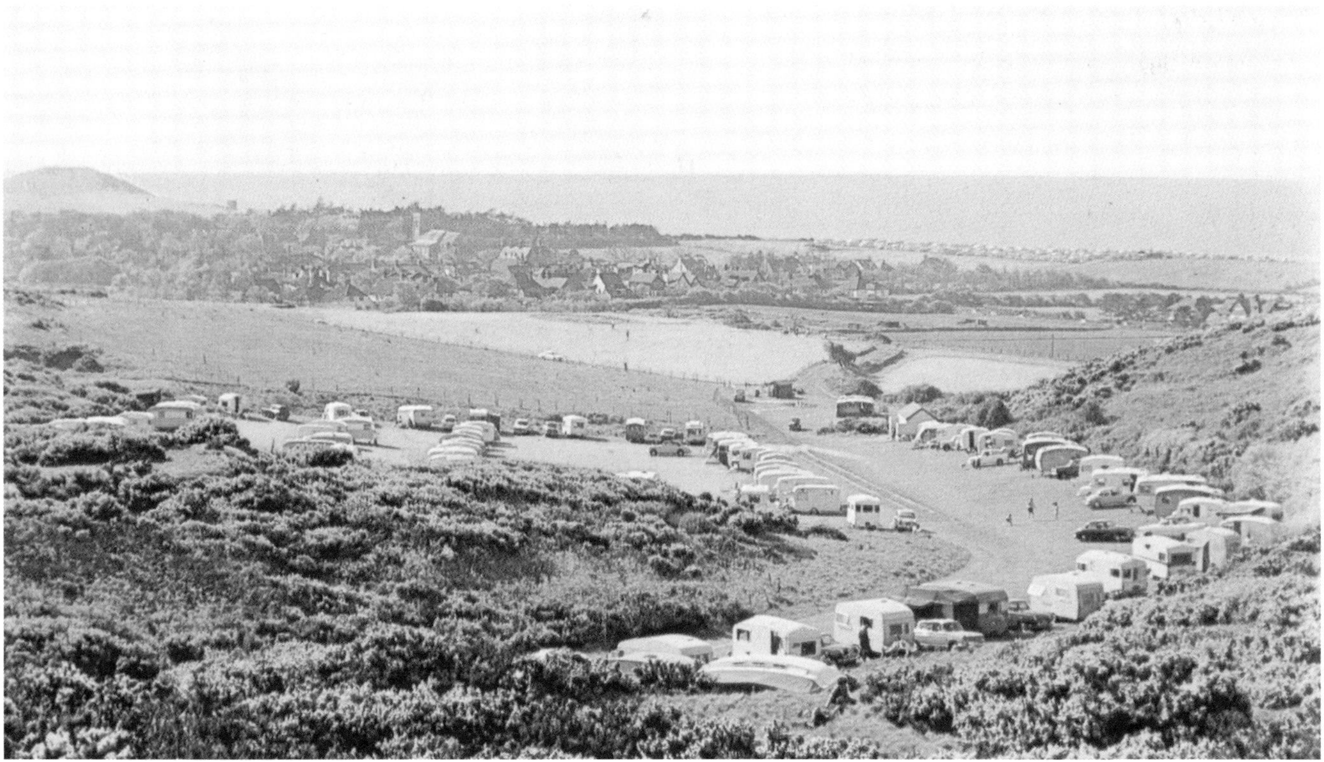

This photograph of East Runton probably dates from around 1900. The chapel, built 1897, shows up well and with part of its predecessor, of 1845, at the rear. Some of the properties immediately beyond it were demolished before much longer and the tall house called Beulah, seen in the recent photograph, was built by G.A.Lines for himself soon after the earlier photograph was taken. It is difficult to see the narrow street, which is now part of the busy A149 road.

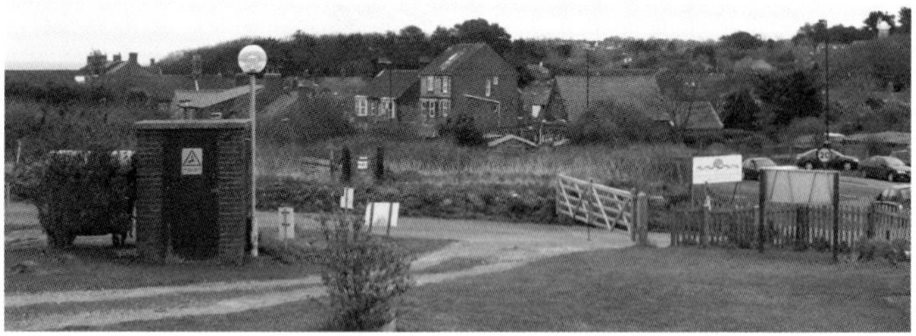

It proved totally impossible to reproduce this view of East Runton because of the many trees that have grown here. The view above is taken from the north side of the coast road and shows the roof of the chapel, the side being obscured by a tree. The white cap of the mill can just be seen on the right but not Cromer Church as in the original photograph, as this is now obscured by the trees to the east of the village.

East Runton - Looking eastwards towards the village

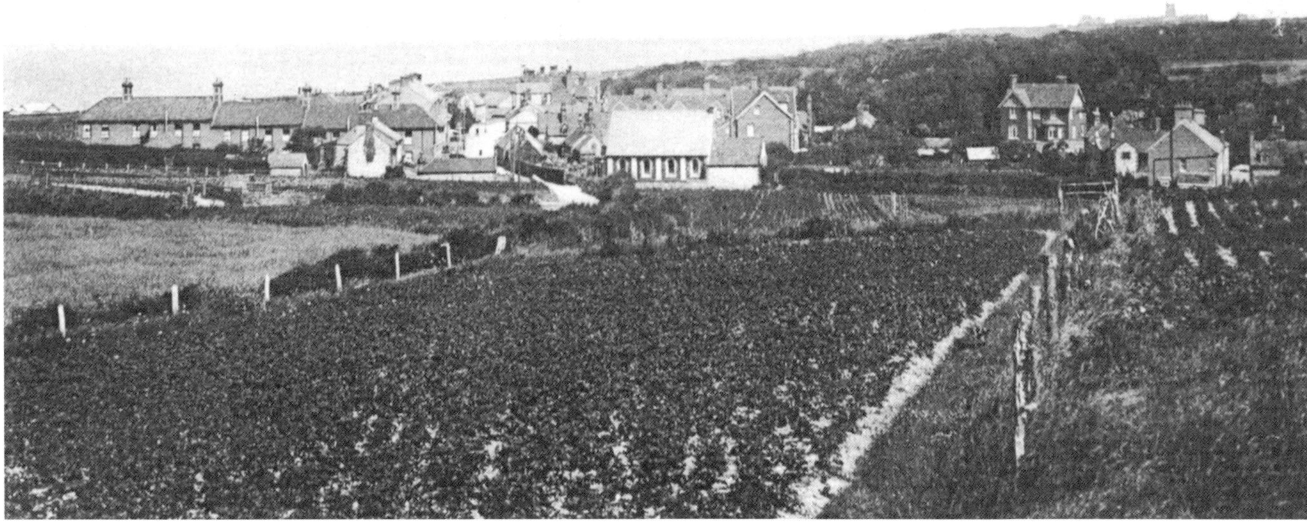

The first reference to the mill at East Runton was in the early 1820's and was probably built by Joseph Baker who married Susan Dawson, whose family owned the local brick works. The mill had four double shuttered sails which drove three pairs of stones. A large detached mill house was built close to the mill. It had a boat shaped cap and a six bladed fan. Records show that it was still working until at least 1908 but was derelict by 1926. The sails and fantail had been removed by 1937 and the cap progressively disappeared in the 1980's. By the 1990's the brick structure had become in poor repair and undoubtedly it would have had to have been demolished had it not been purchased and turned into a fine award winning home in 2000. The photographs opposite show the mill in 1890 and with the mill house in 1909.

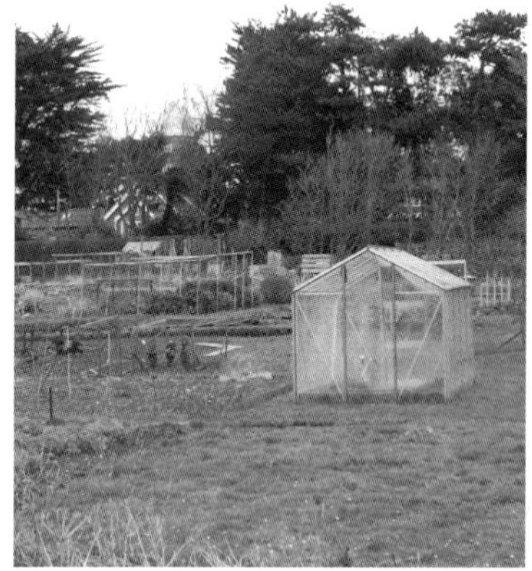

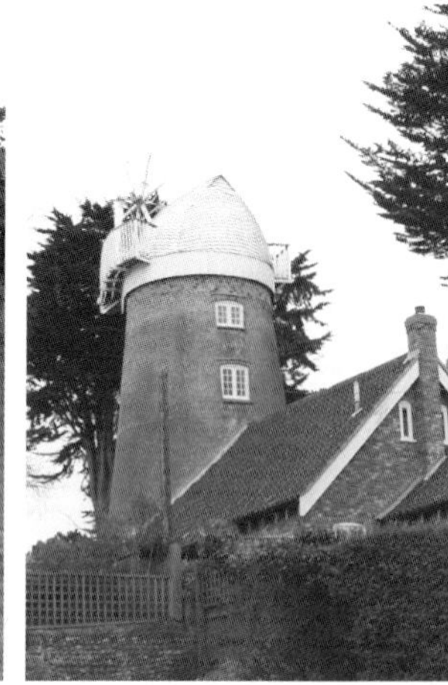

The restoration of the mill included the construction of a new cap and six bladed fan but not sails. It is not possible to reproduce the eastward looking view of the mill across what are now allotments, because of the large trees that have grown up. The mill can just be seen in the gap in the trees above, but the mill house is totally hidden by them. The old view on the right, showing the west facing front of Mill House, cannot be replicated as this is now the rear of the house and trees obscure both the house and the mill.

East Runton - The Mill

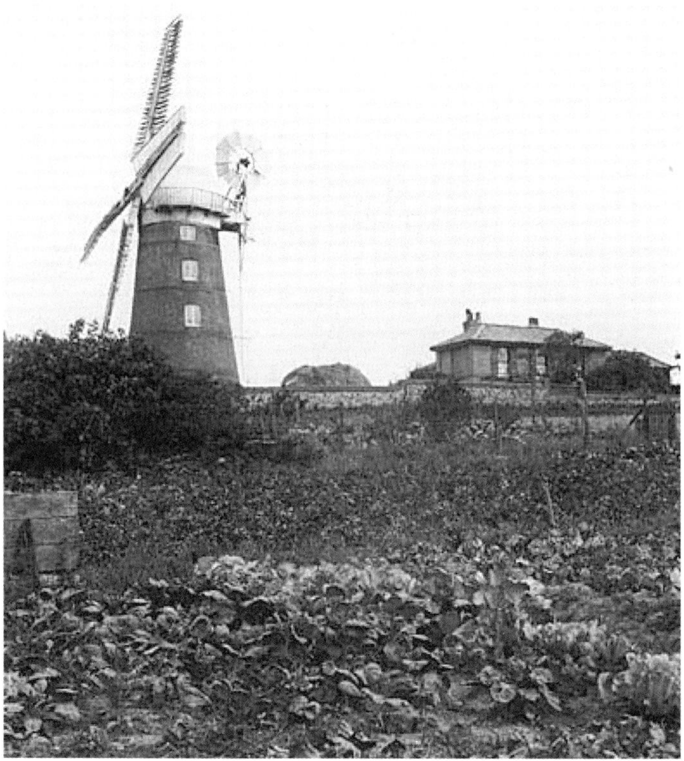

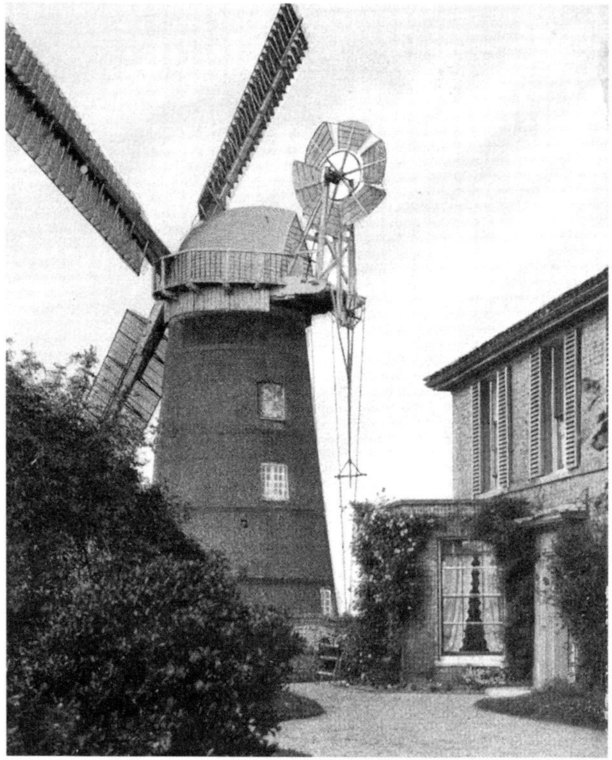

Both East and and West Runton had a brick yard, as did most villages. The reason being that in the early days of building houses of brick, there was no way of conveying large amounts of what would have been a very heavy commodity over long distances. The one pictured opposite, with the smoke indicating that a firing was taking place, was owned by Gunton Brothers, who had several brickyards in the county. The remains of this kiln can still be seen today, incorporated into a newer building on the north side of the road between East and West Runton. The clay for the bricks was dug from a pit beside the kiln. The brickworks at East Runton were located in Brick Lane, adjacent to the Old Hall. The West Runton works were closed just before the second world war, while the one at East Runton closed down in 1951. The bricks from the demolition of this kiln were utilised in building the chalets at Poplars holiday park which was built on the site.

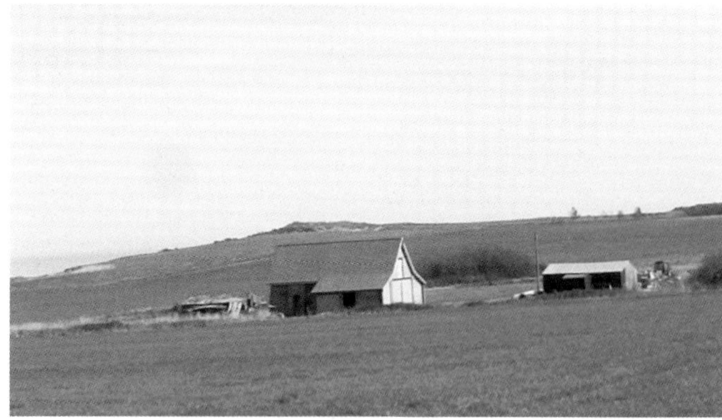

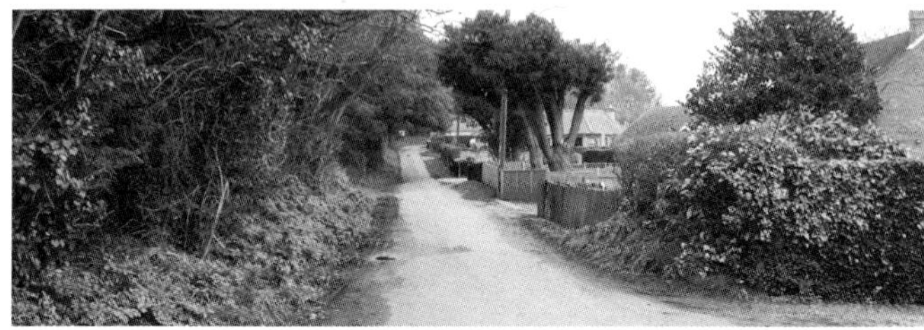

The top picture is the site today of the brick works pictured opposite and the lower picture is the present view, looking down Brick Lane in East Runton.

West and East Runton - Brick Works

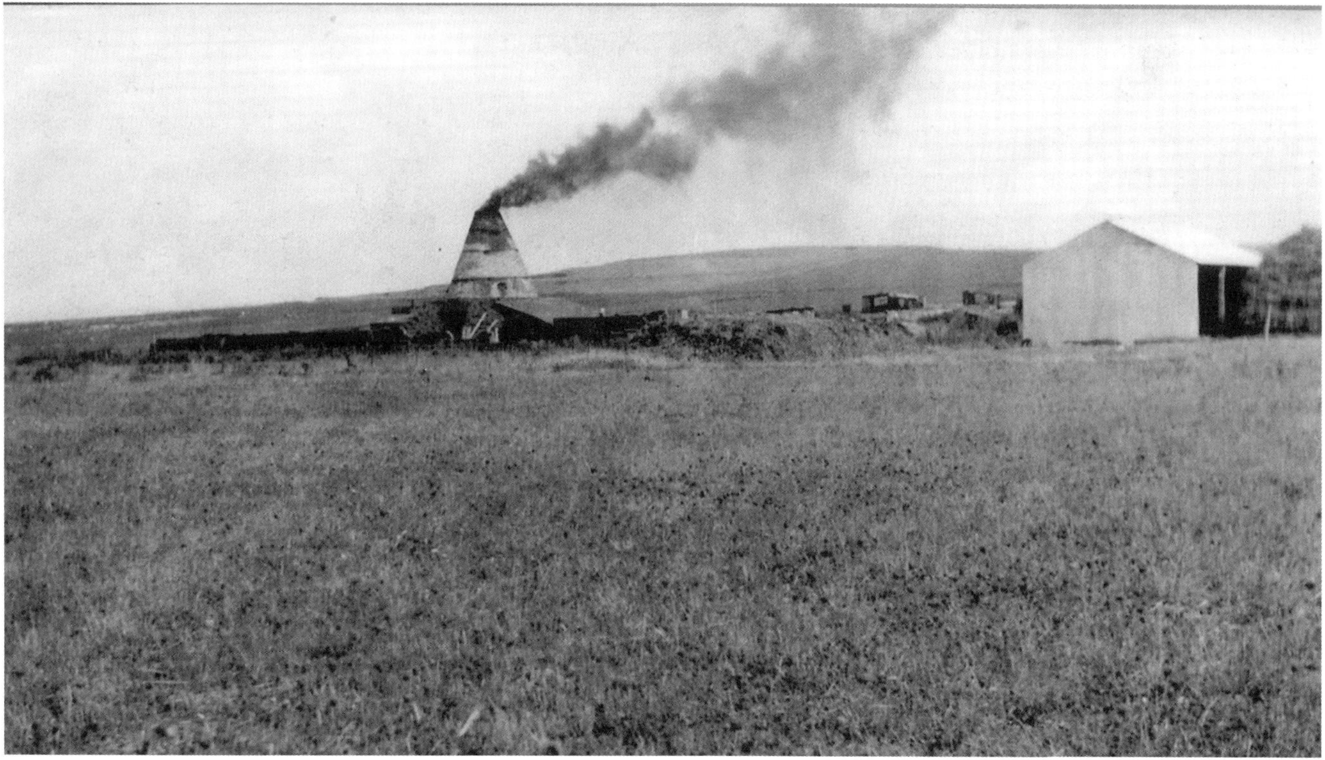

The railway carrying passengers from the midlands via South Lynn and Fakenham to a new station at Cromer arrived in 1887. In 1906 a spur was built from a junction by the bridge at the top of Thains Lane East Runton, to enable trains to travel to Norwich and London without having to first call at the Cromer station, thus saving time. This involved the construction of a viaduct just south of the the one which stands by the village hall. Apparently the soil for the construction of the embankments on the approaches to the viaduct was transported by rail from Newmarket where a cutting for another stretch of track was being excavated. On 21st April 1963, this line was closed, but the viaduct still lives on as a memorial to what must have been a very exciting time for the inhabitants of East and West Runton.

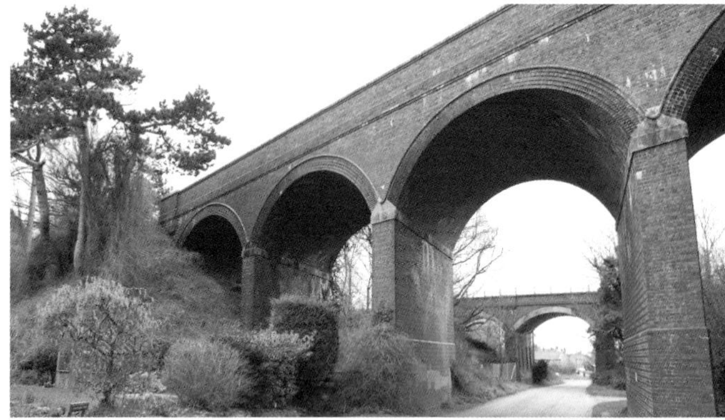

When you next pass under the railway viaducts at East Runton, do take time to stop and refect on what impressive structures they are. Given that they were built using such simple equipment as the wooden hand operated hoists and the wheelbarrows shown in this fascinating photograph.

East Runton - Railway Viaduct

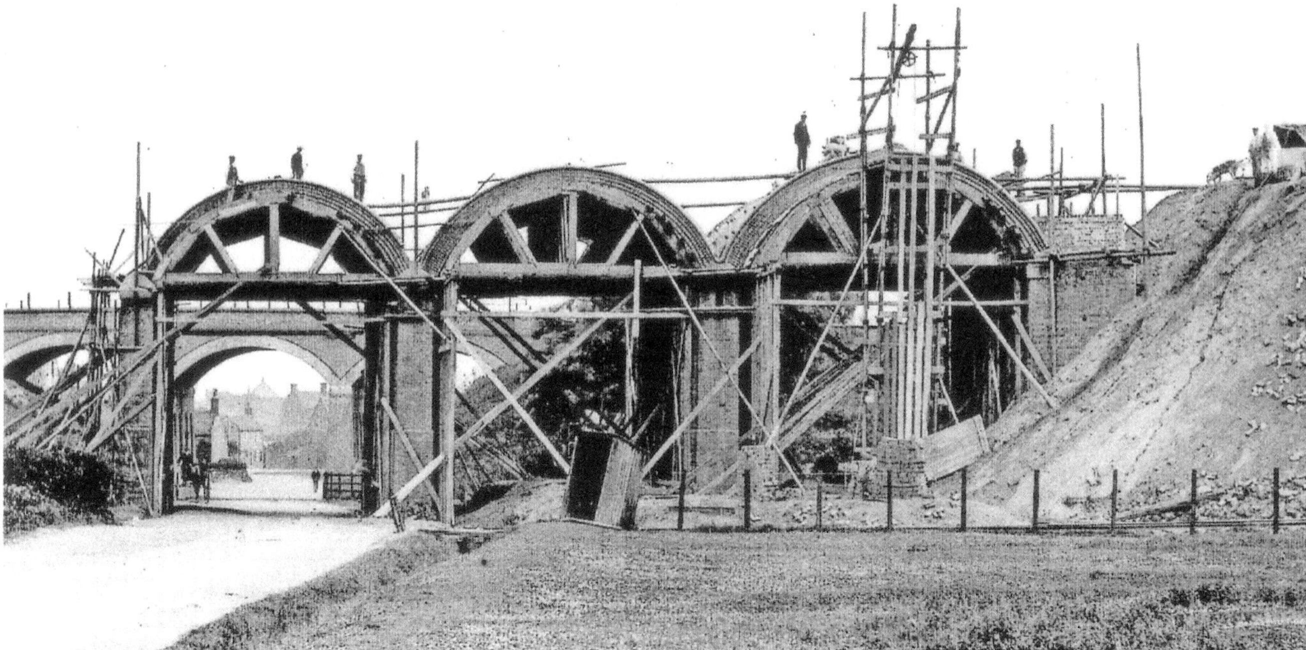

This view of the railway viaduct is of around 1950. The construction of the railway embankment across the valley in which East Runton lies altered the landscape considerably. The five arch viaduct came into use in 1906 and closed to rail traffic in 1963. The three arch bridge beyond it dates from 1887 and remains in use today.

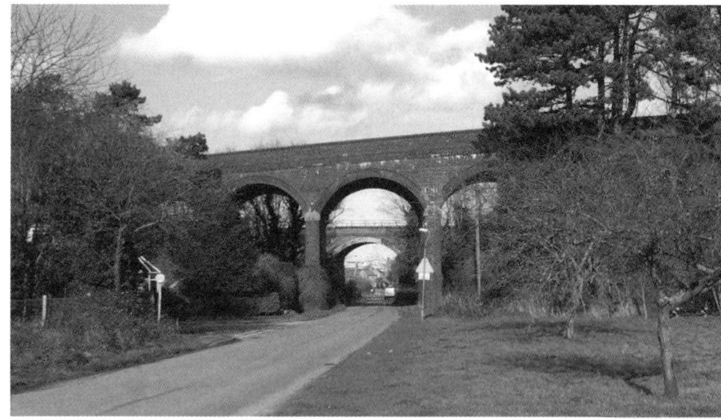

The recent view is not markedly different, save that the trees and vegetation have grown up and the embankments are no longer maintained and kept clear of the growth as they were in the days of steam trains.

East Runton - Railway Viaduct

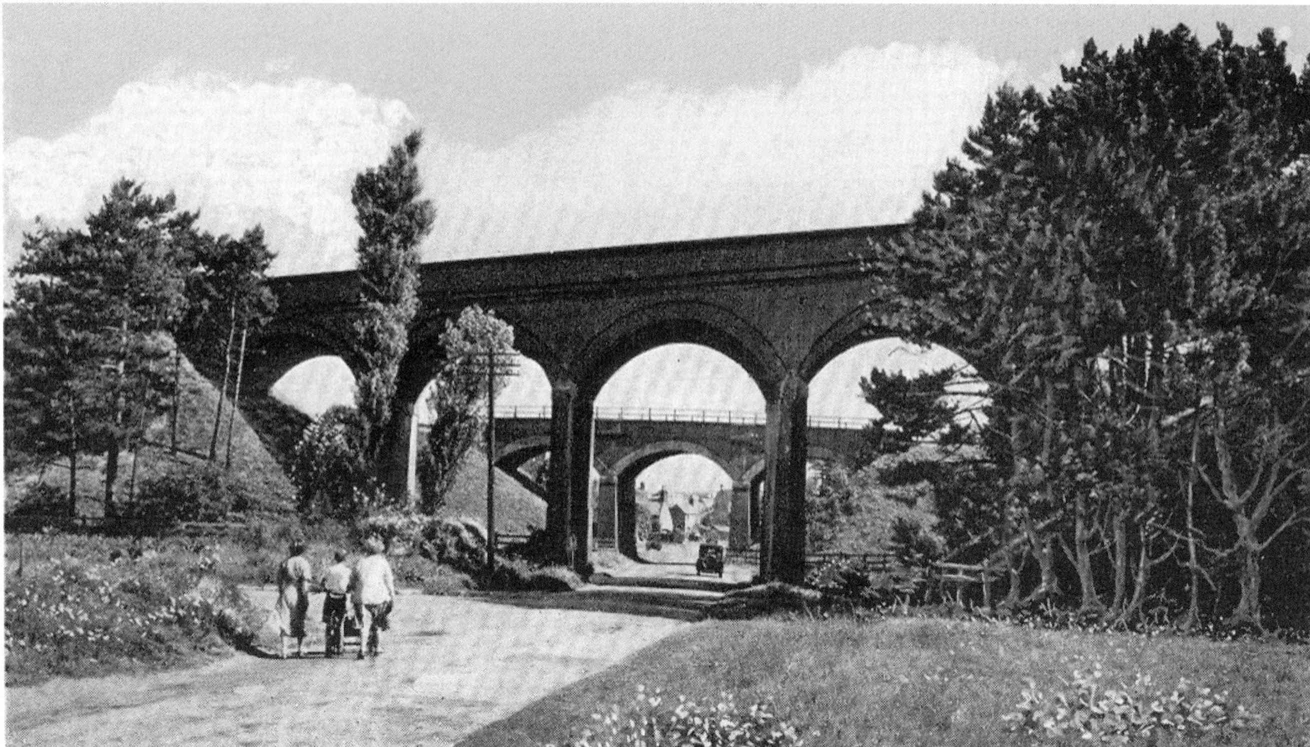

The railway came through Runton, altering considerably the landscape of both both villages, in 1887. West Runton Station was opened in September 1887, three months after the line to Cromer had opened. Although a double track was allowed for it was only ever a single track.. The long platform at a humble station was required for the trains which came from the Midlands bringing holiday-makers.The station buildings planned for, with Station Masters house, were never built and for the whole period the station was staffed it had only this "temporary" building, with a disused freight van later added for bicycles, etc. The name board has recently (2011) been restored. The criss-cross fencing was a feature of the Midland & Great Northern railway. The line had begun as the Eastern & Midlands railway. The view of the station on the opposite page is of the 1920's.

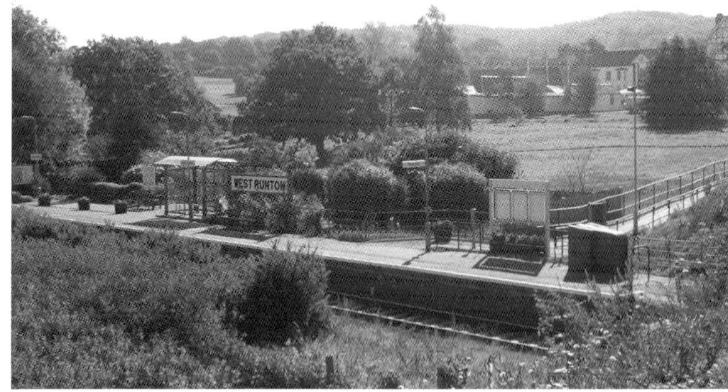

Today West Runton station is on the line from Norwich to Sheringham which is known as the Bittern Line. A recent link across the road in Sheringham, allows trains from Norwich to access the Poppy Line of the North Norfolk Railway from Sheringham to Holt. This means that once again steam locomatives can occasionally be seen passing through West Runton station enroute to visiting the Poppy Line.

West Runton - Railway Station

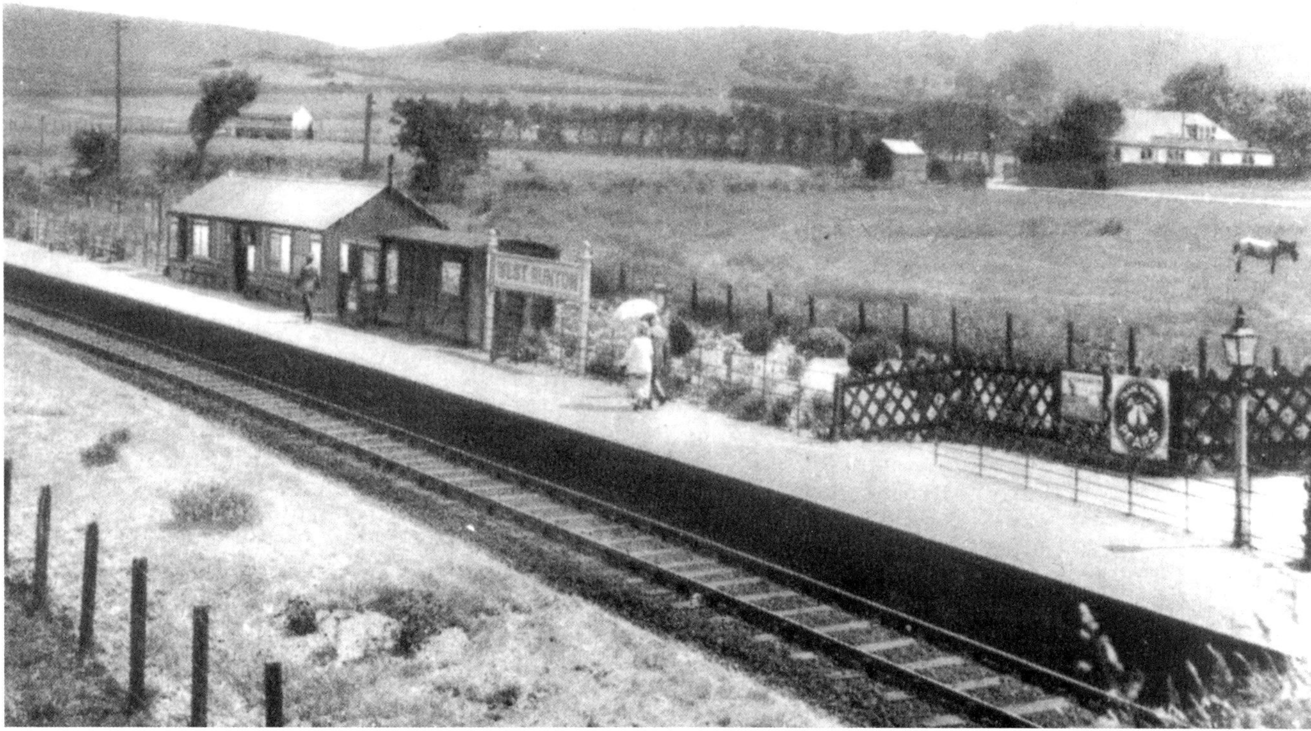

A view of the Lower Common at East Runton of around 1950, though it had changed little in the preceding twenty years. The flint cottages are difficult to date.

Looking at the end wall of the cottages in the left front it can be seen that this has been heightened, as the former gable line shows, probably an improvement of the 1840's when the Buxton family acquired much of East Runton.

We know that the young children in the photograph are Carl Hodson and his sister Eileen. Carl still lives in East Runton.

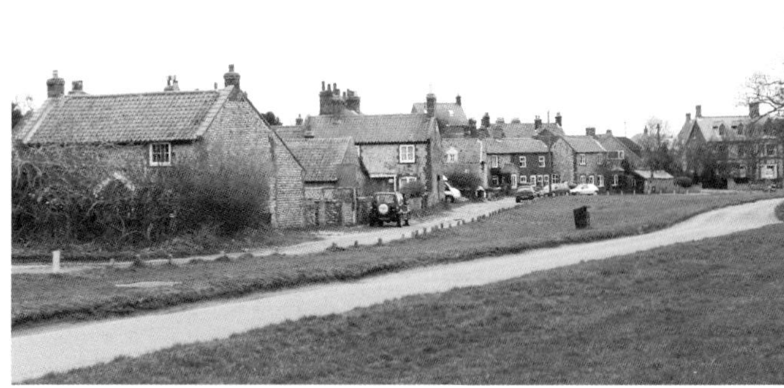

In the recent view the cottages are the same but have all been smartened up and here and there different windows may be seen, also a new garage gable. There were no cars parked in 1950, as now, and there is a line of concrete posts, erected by the council in 1965, to impede parking on the Common. Some trees have grown up in the background and the tall house in the High Street, Beulah, shows above the roof tops. Along the Common can be seen the path created by pedestrian usage and for which there was formerly no need.

East Runton - Lower Common, looking north.

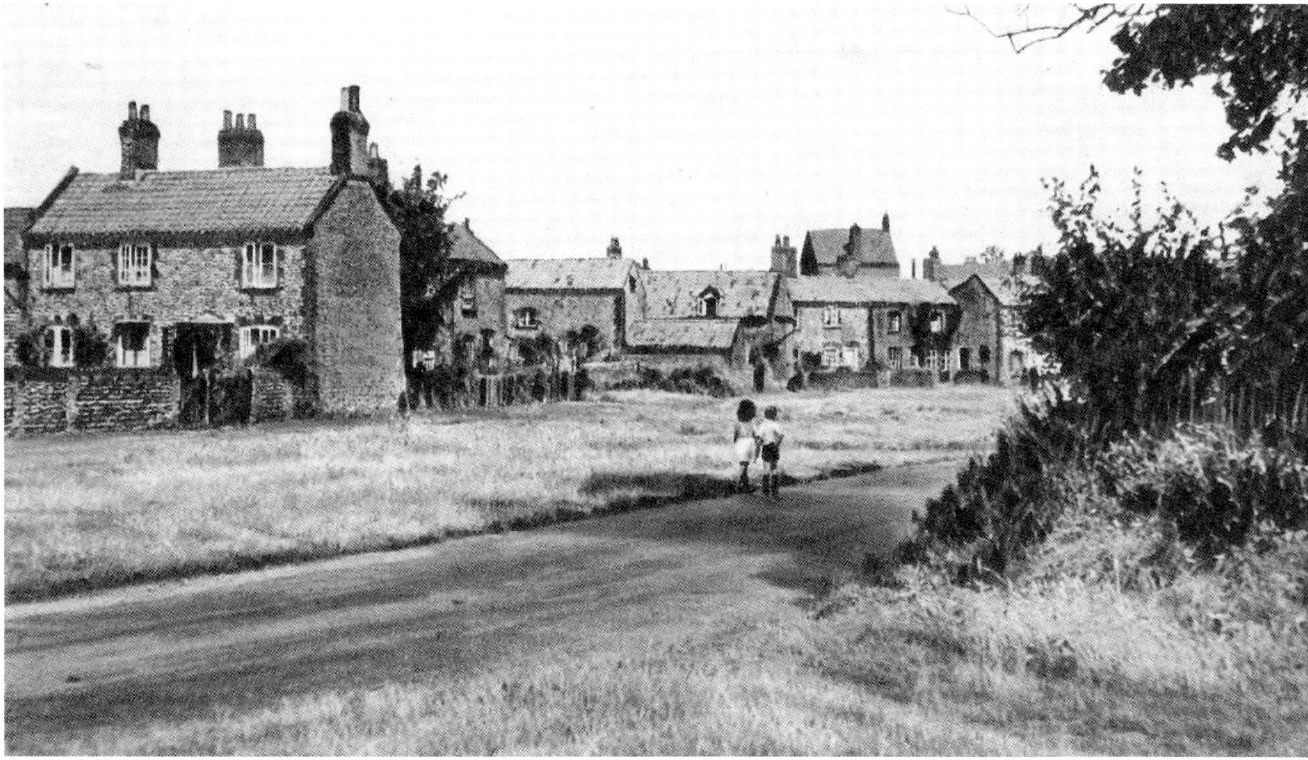

This view of the Lower Common Pond, looking south dates from the early years of the last century, prior to 1906, the year in which a cottage was added on the north end of the pair in the centre of the view. The pond, really a watering place for cattle and horses, was then smaller than now and the area of grass was much less.. On the skyline at the rear is the roof of the village school with its bell-cot on the gable. It could be that the children around the pond had been gathered from the school with a teacher.

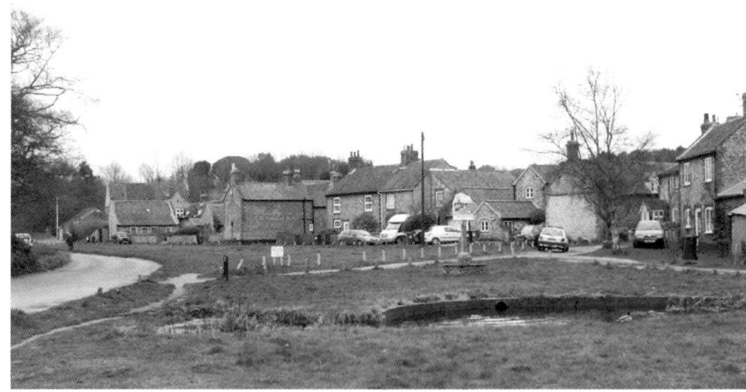

The recent view shows more grass on the Common and a path where the entrance of the pond has been closed off. No children are visible, but cars are parked on the track in front of the cottages.

East Runton - Lower Common, looking south.

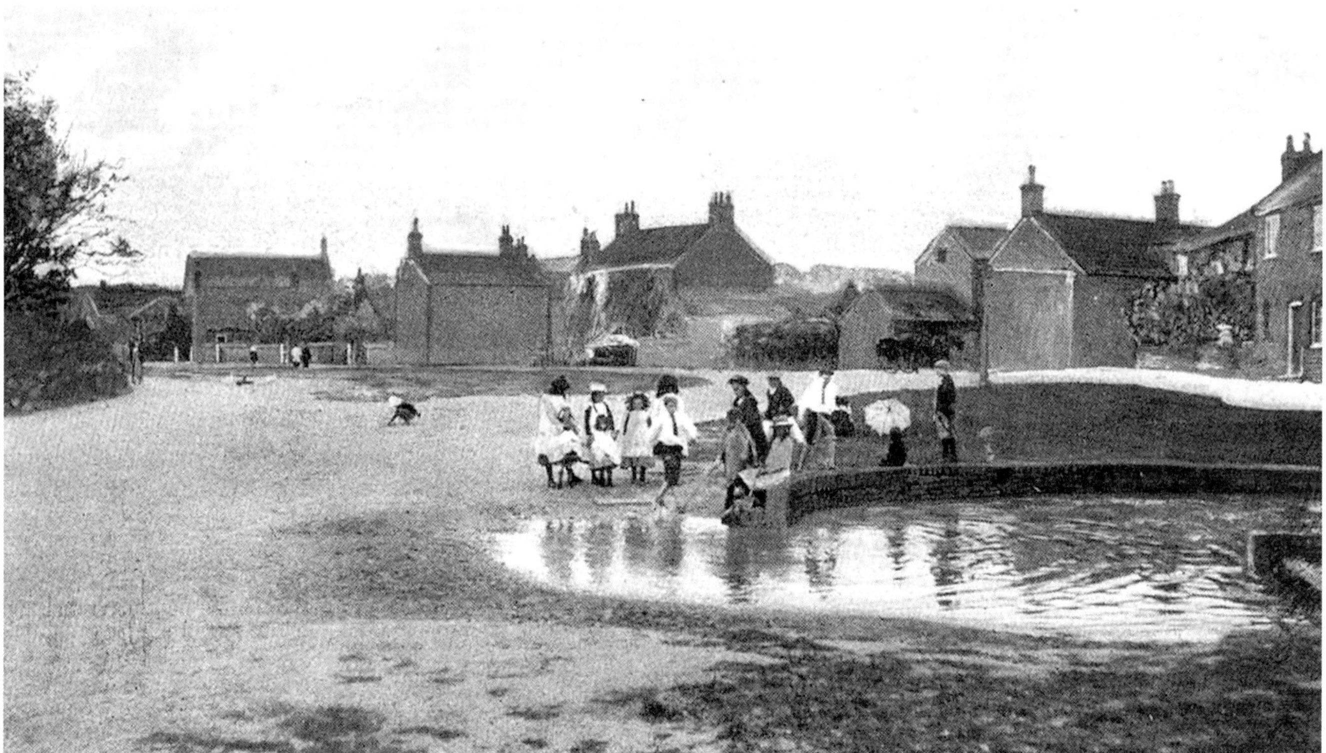

This view dates from before 1910. There were then no plants around the pond and any curbing was minimal. The row of five cottages was built in 1898, the other properties shown are much older.

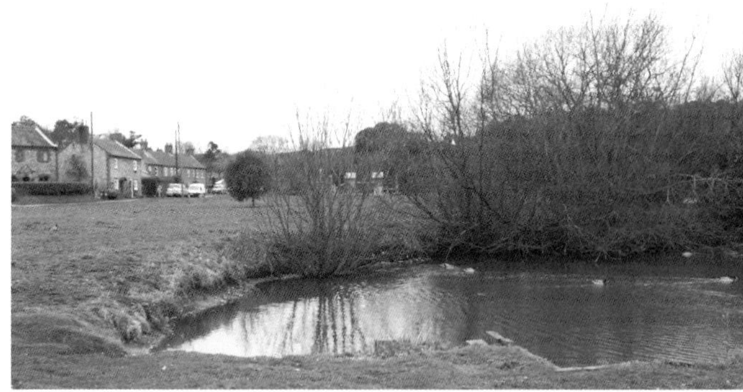

The present day view has been taken looking across the southern edge of the pond, so that the total view was not obscured by the shrubs and trees on the west side of the pond. A plaque on a post amongst these trees commemorates their planting by pupils of Cromer Junior School in the winter of 1990/91

East Runton - Top Common, looking west.

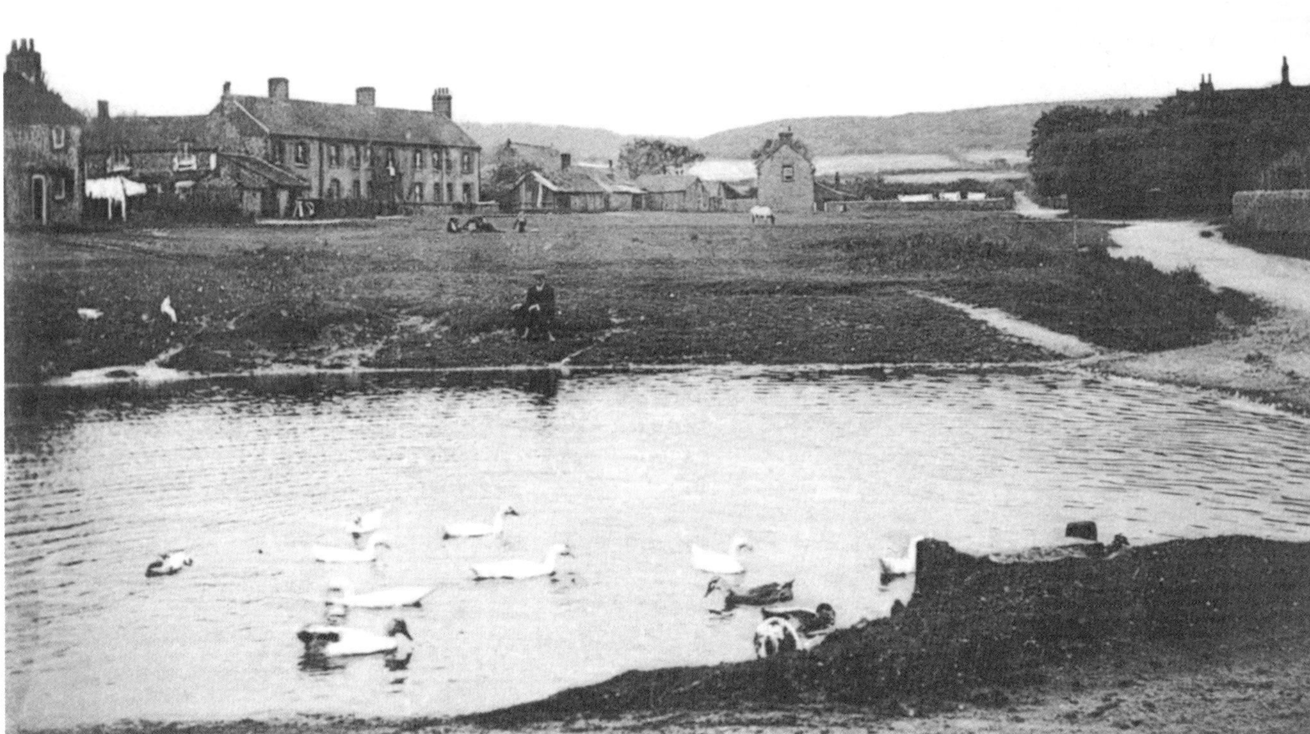

This view across the Top Common Pond at East Runton, looking north, is difficult to date but is probably not later than 1920. What the property on the right of the photograph is, no one seems to remember. The house now on the site was built by G. A. Lines in the early 1920's. The meadow behind the people standing in the road, is now the site of the post - 1945 housing estate named Buxton Close. Notice that there are no rails around the pond - this is before the days of Health and Safety.

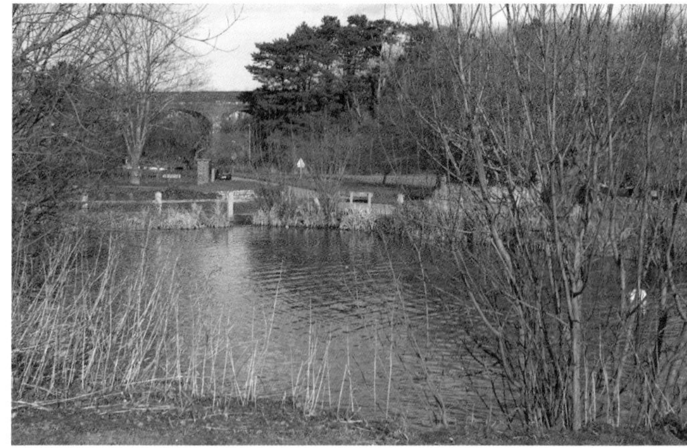

The current picture shows the vegetation which has grown up around the pond. Behind it can just be seen one of the houses of Buxton Close. There are now barriers around the road edges.

East Runton - view north across the pond on Top Common

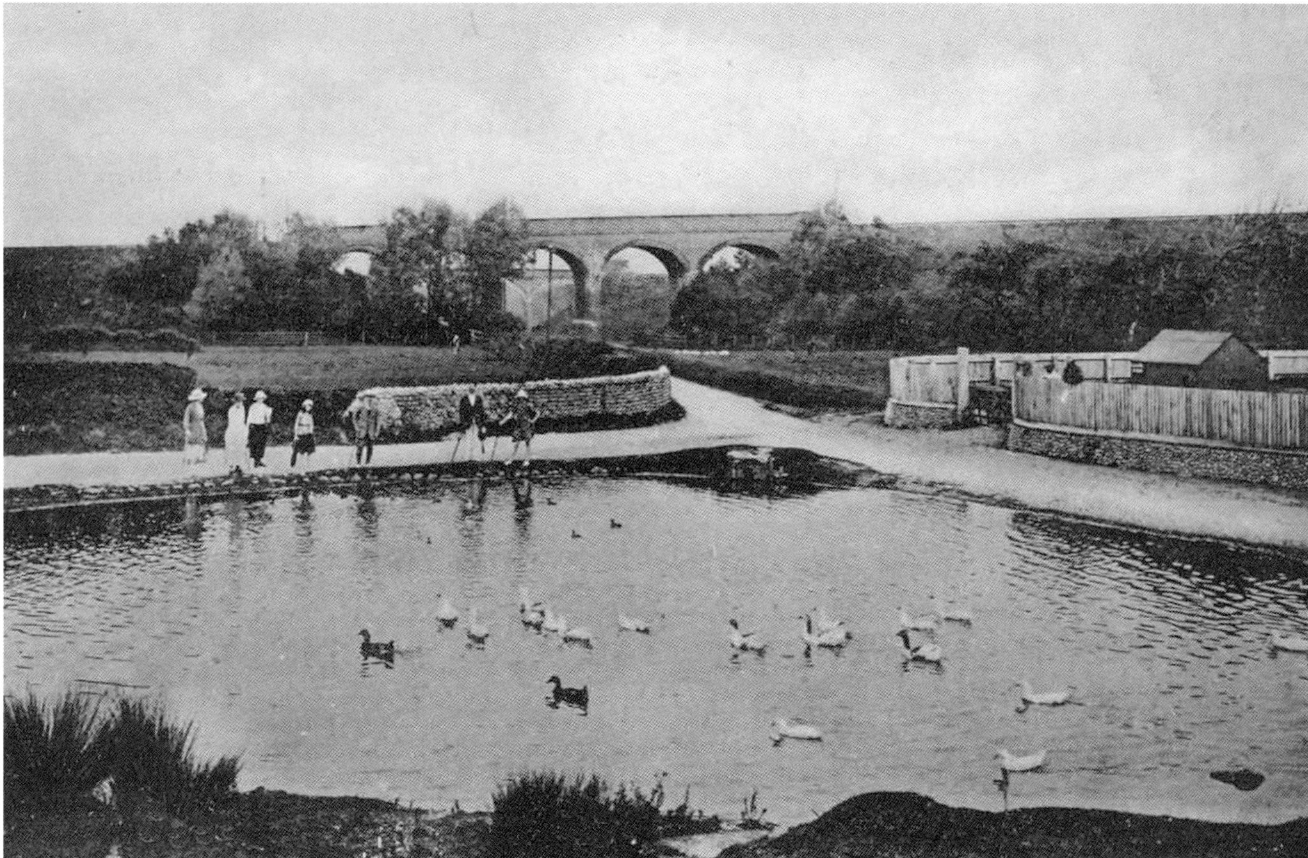

This view of West Runton Common opposite is pre-1914 but only just. The pond, fed by the stream which comes down from the hills and finally reaches the beach, had not yet been curbed. It was made as a watering hole for cattle and horses, with a sloped entrance, no longer apparent. In front of the houses to the right can be seen a pump, still there but no longer working, from which Spring Cottages, the row to the left, obtained their water. During the 1939-45 War the military obtained supplies of water from this source. A car from the period stands under the trees. The top view on this page is from the 1920's. The pond now has walls around it of flintstone. The house on the left, Wood Rising, was built in 1911 by the architect W.A. Forsyth as a holiday house for himself and family. He later sold it and restored the Church Farm House. There is again a car parked by the trees.
The lower picture was taken recently.

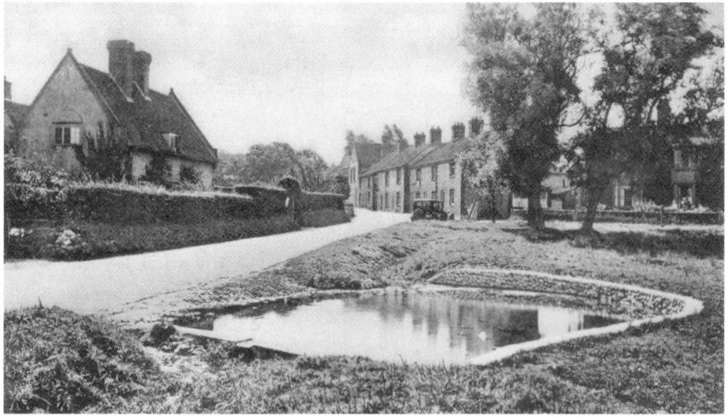

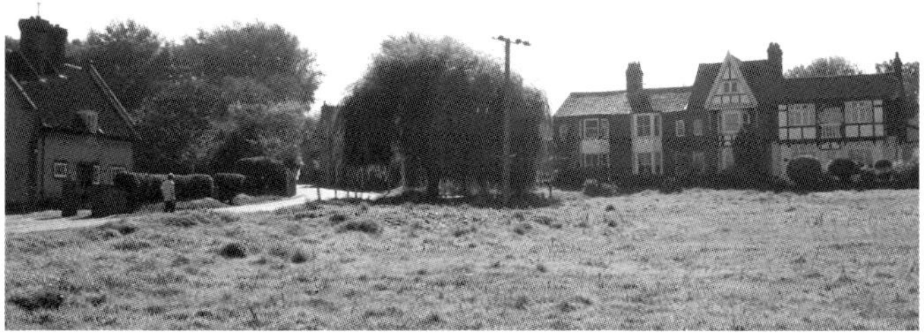

West Runton - The Common.

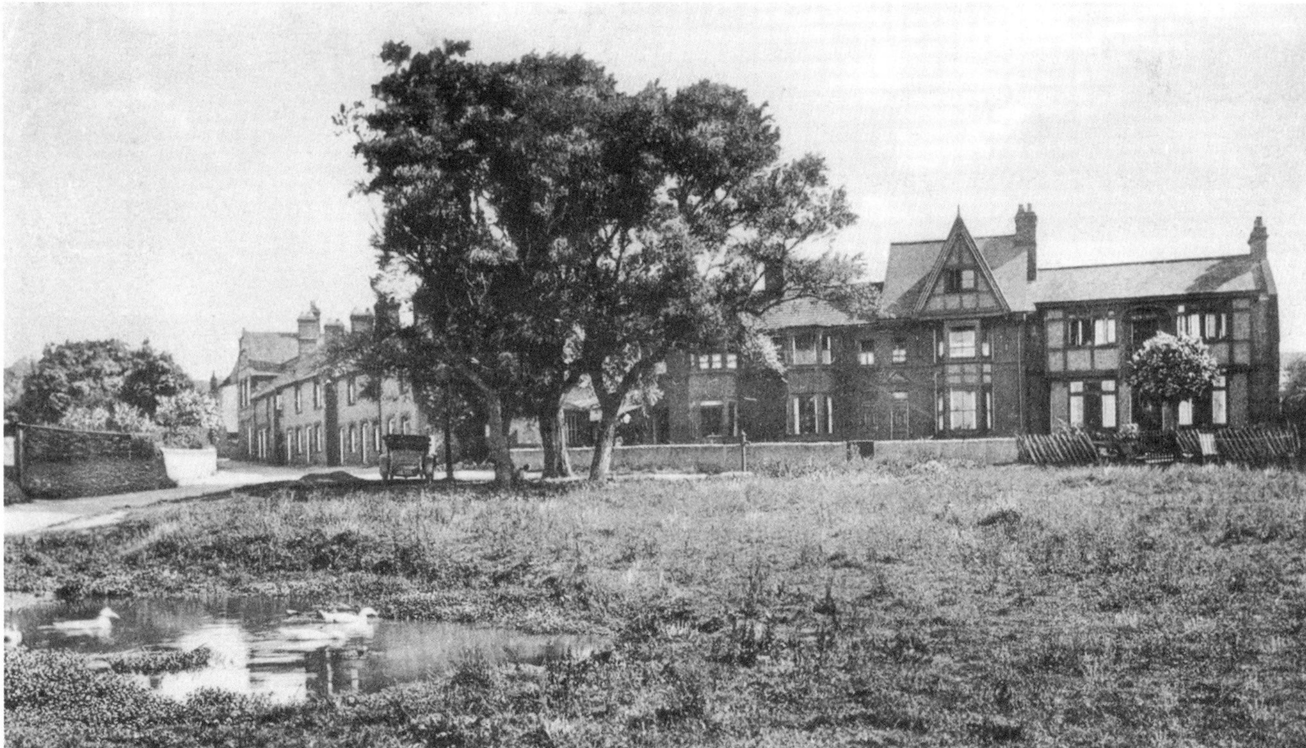

This view of East Runton Gap is typical of many. It is taken from a postcard that was posted in August 1922, but the view probably dates from 1920. At this time the gap is an unmade track, fishing boats are lying up it, and holiday makers are going up and down it. At the bottom are two huts, used by tent and deckchair hirers when not used for fishing gear. The Gap is said to have been scoured by the Great Flood of 1912. It is low tide, there are fishing boats on the sand and areas of sand uncovered by the ebbing tide.

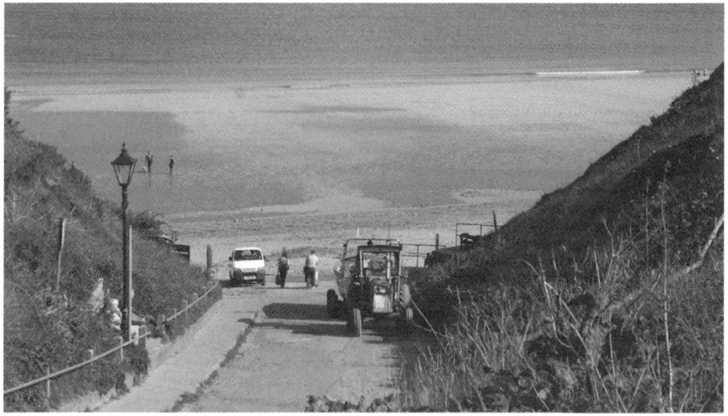

The present day view shows the access to the beach now concreted, the path on the left pre-dates the rest of the track. Banks are now grassed and the one on the left is much less steep - defences are now in place here to stop the erosion that has taken place since the 1920's photograph.There is still a fishing boat in the picture but now hauled up with the help of a tractor. Other modern developments in the picture include the street light and the fisherman's truck.

East Runton - Gap

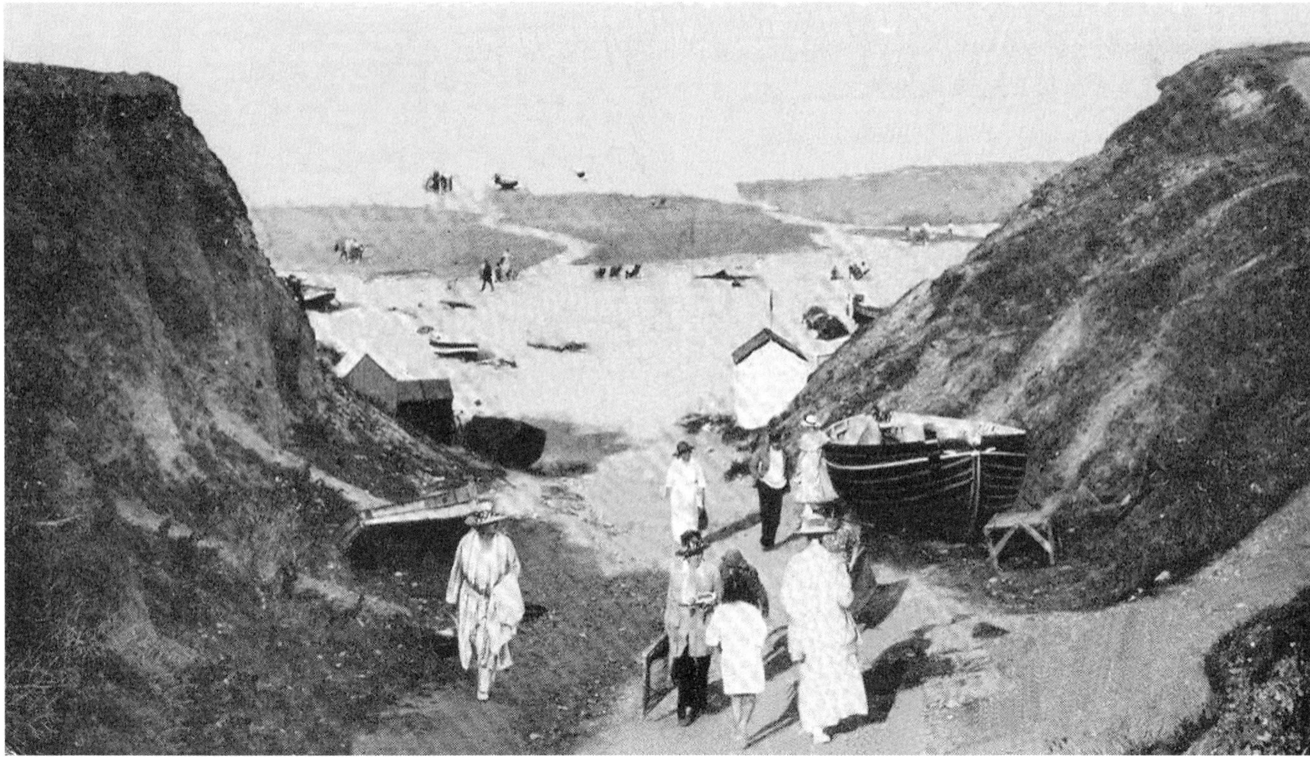

The photograph opposite encompases the beach, the Gap and the clifftop at East Runton. It is difficult to date precisely but the design of the caravans suggest that it was taken in the sixties or seventies. There were no beach huts at East Runton after the end of the seventies. The huts were mostly owned by fishermen and were erected each year for the summer season and removed over the winter.

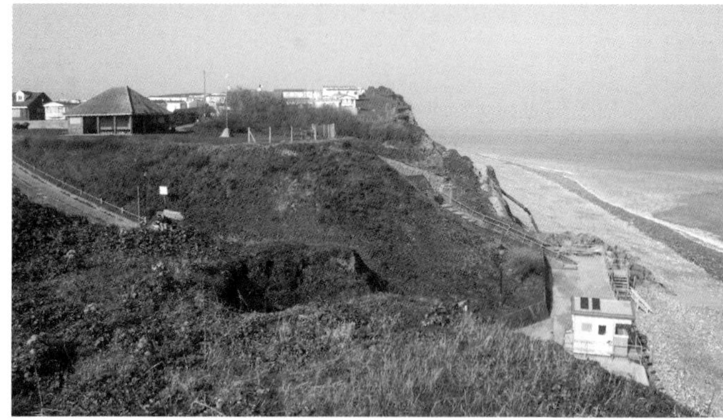

It was difficult to get to a similar vantage point to take the current photograph, although the photographer does admit to straying over the cliff-top barrier. It actually appears as if the original photograph was taken part of the way down the cliff. There will have been some erosion since the sixties, but less here because of sea defences around the gap. The only hut that can be seen today is the one belonging to the RNLI's lifeguards.

East Runton - Cliffs and beach

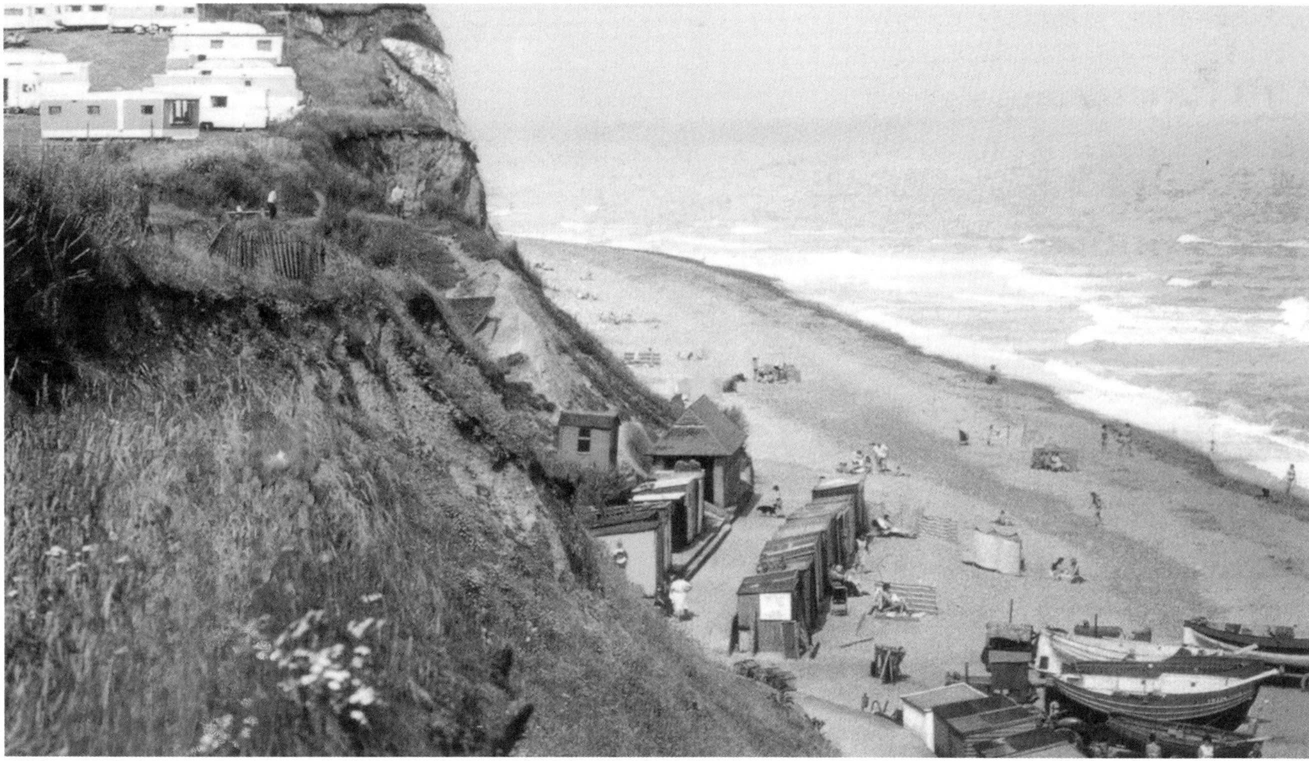

An August scene of anytime between about 1925 and 1935. It shows the line of tents which were a summer feature of both Runton villages. Here donkeys are waiting to give rides to children. They are probably Walter "Nipper" Tuck's. There is a fine expanse of sand and a black line of seaweed brought in by the tide, known locally as a sea harvest. The houses of Cromer are creeping nearer to East Runton. A wide clifftop footpath can be seen with people walking to and from Cromer.

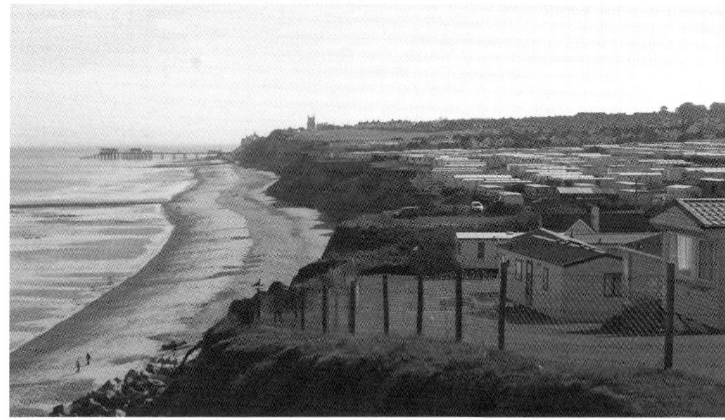

No doubt the cliffs have eroded several metres in the eighty years between these two photographs, but there is no way of readily seeing this. The main difference is the large number of static caravans, which now occupy the cliff top on both sides of the East Runton gap. There is no path along the clifftop to Cromer.

East Runton - Beach and cliffs

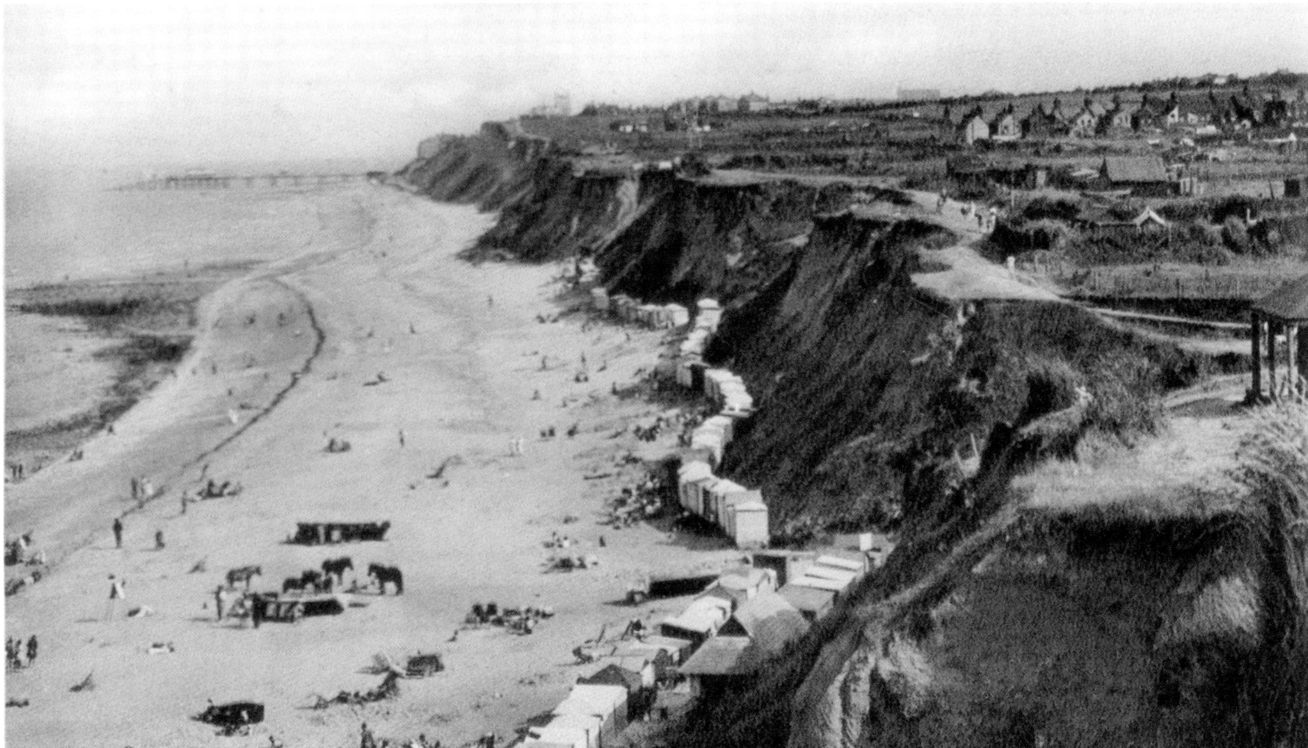

At the top of the road leading now to the Laburnum Caravan Site at West Runton, on the right hand side, was formerly a lime kiln. The chalk burnt in this to produce lime was gathered from the beach and this pathway, long lost to the sea, was used for access to the beach - the chalk being transported by horse and cart. In the photograph you can see a man, sitting reading, in the lower right hand corner. Herbert Love, known as "Darby" was killed on this path in 1913 whilst going up or down with a cart. He may be the man shown here.

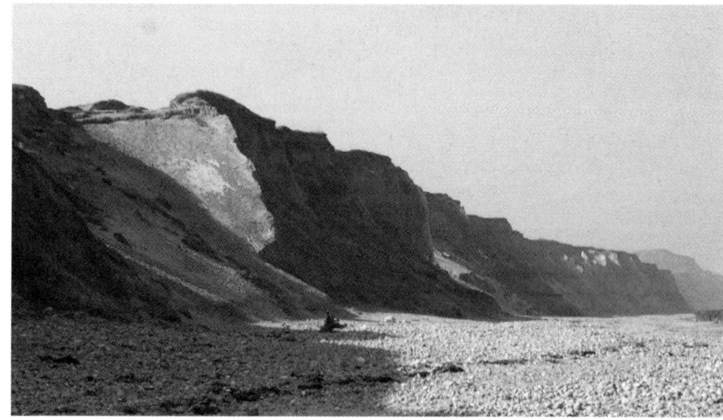

The track down to the beach would have been along this section of the coast, but of course closer to the sea, allowing for the amount of erosion that has taken place over the past 100 years. Nonetheless one can imagine and admire the men whose job was to transport chalk up these cliffs by horse and cart.

West Runton - Beach and cliffs

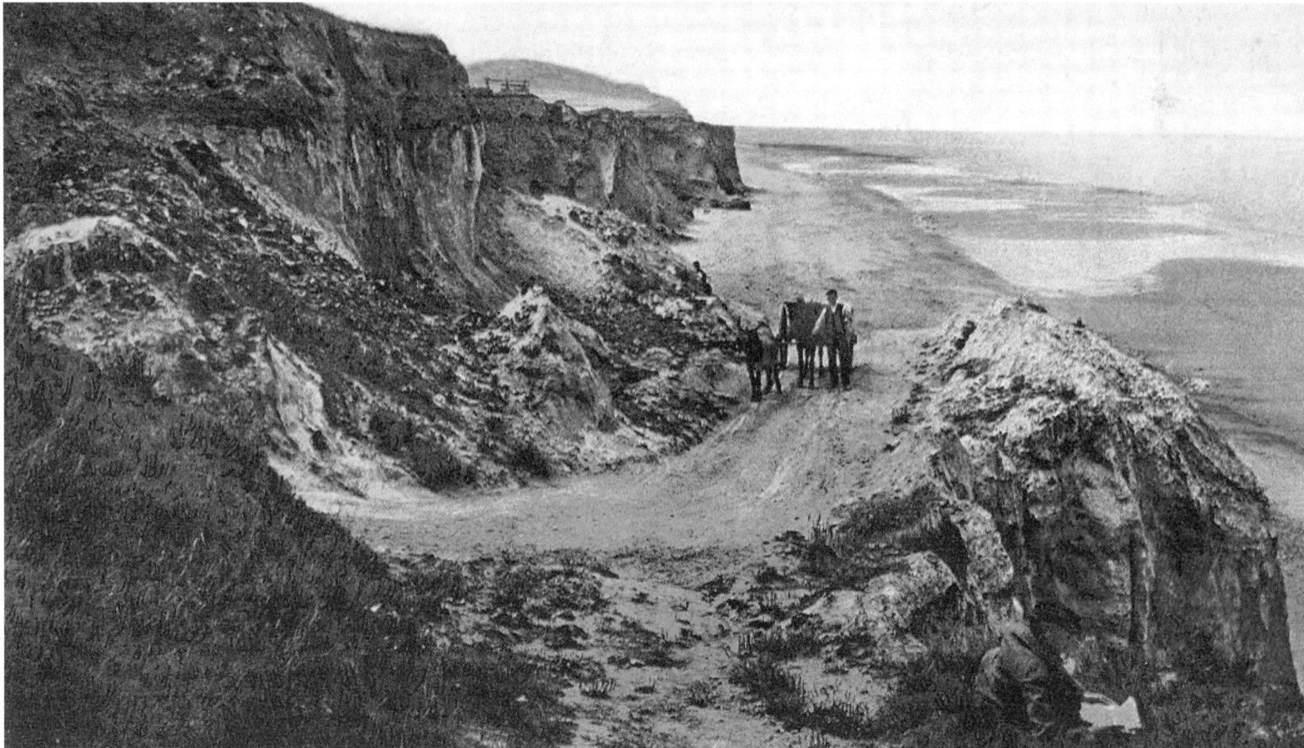

This is from a series of views still on sale in 1923 but taken some years previously. This shows what is probably the first refreshment hut. On the immediate right is West Runton's first sewage treatment works. The ventilation pipe was subsequently removed and the iron railings succumbed to years of salt spray.

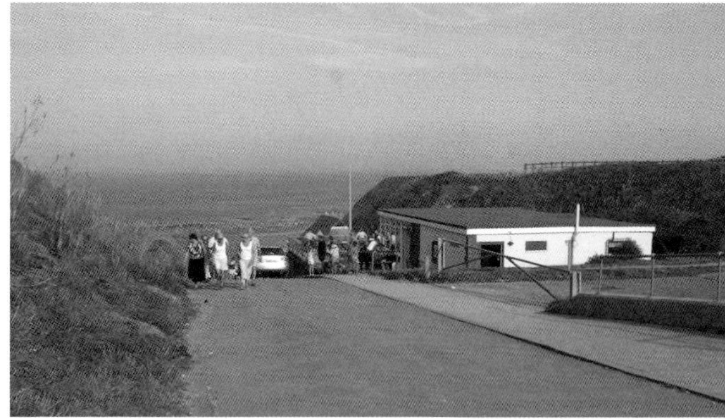

The Gap has changed little in the 80+ years since the original photograph, except that the refreshment building is now of more substantial construction. The cliffs just to the east of here became the centre of attention in the 1990's, when the West Runton Elephant was excavated. It proved to be the largest fossil elephant skeleton ever to have been found in Britain .

West Runton - Gap

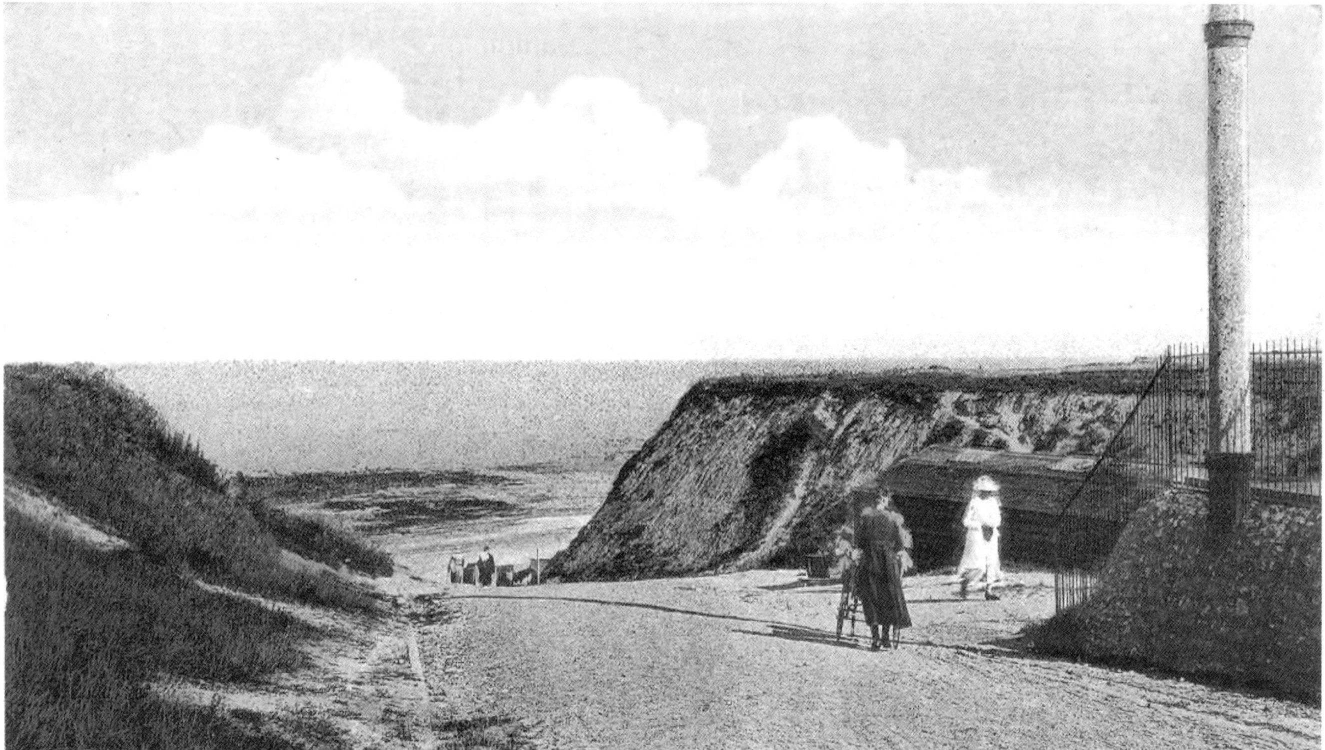

This is a view from the mid-1930's. The Willow Cove Cafe, which had a succession of owners, closed at the end of the season in 1939. It was burnt down during the War when a fire lit by soldiers in a stove got out of hand and consumed the premises. Below the Cafe can be seen the Public Conveniences, now somewhat updated from their first building, and beyond them the huts of those who hired tents and deck chairs. The path down the Gap had been concreted by this time, but the rest of the slope was not made up until around 1950.

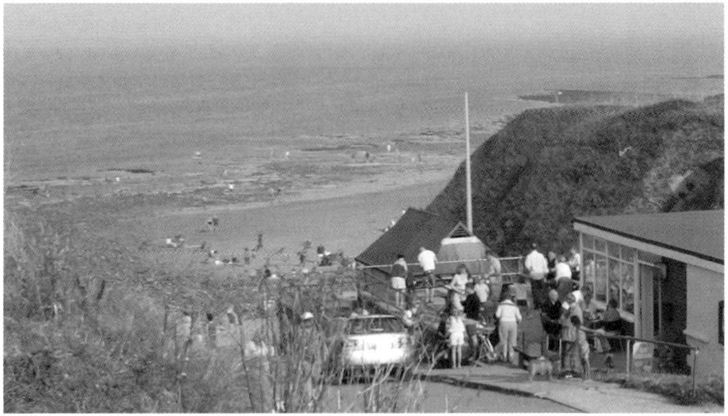

The Willow Cove Cafe has been replaced by the Seaview Beach Cafe which continues in the tradition of providing refreshment to the many visitors. Louise, the proprietor has an unusual collection of fossils from the nearby cliffs and also an interesting collection of old postcards of West Runton.

West Runton - Gap and Willow Cove Cafe

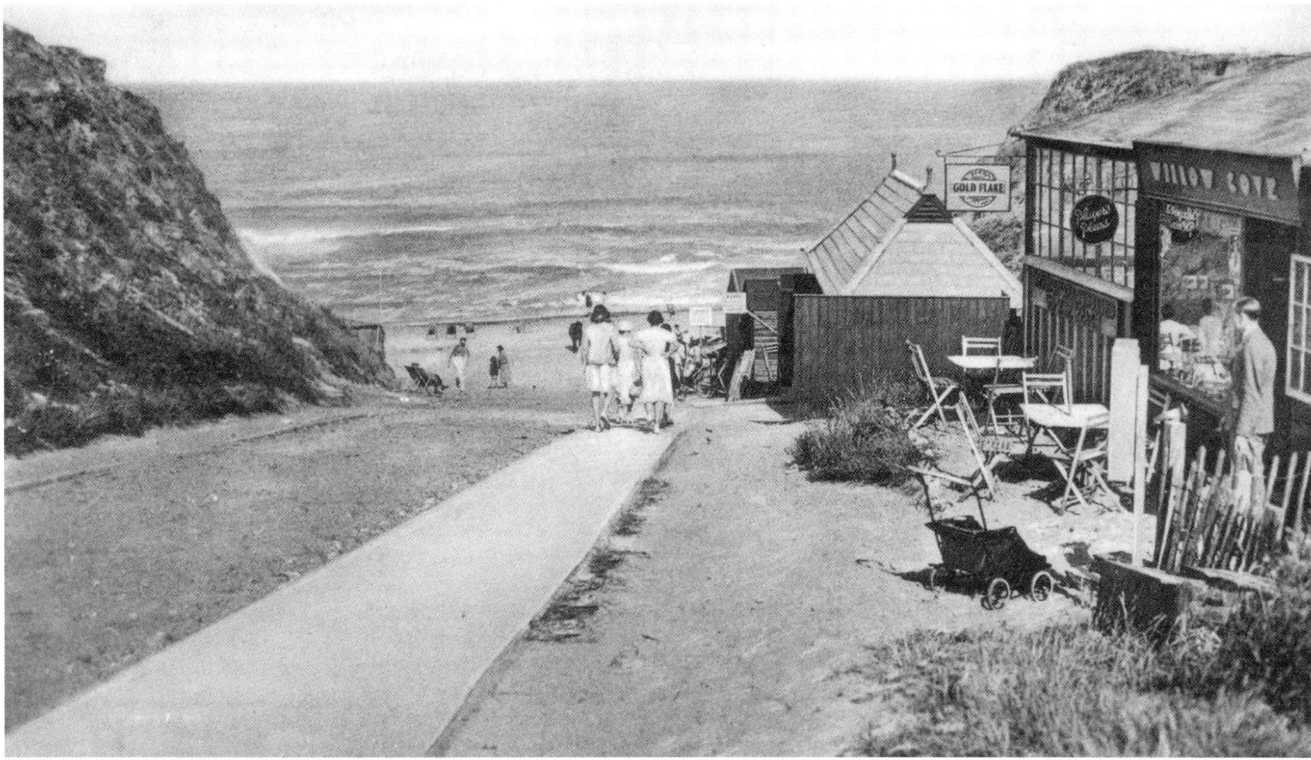

Printed by Barnwell Print Ltd, Aylsham, Norfolk